AUTOBIOGRAPHY OF PETER TAYLOR

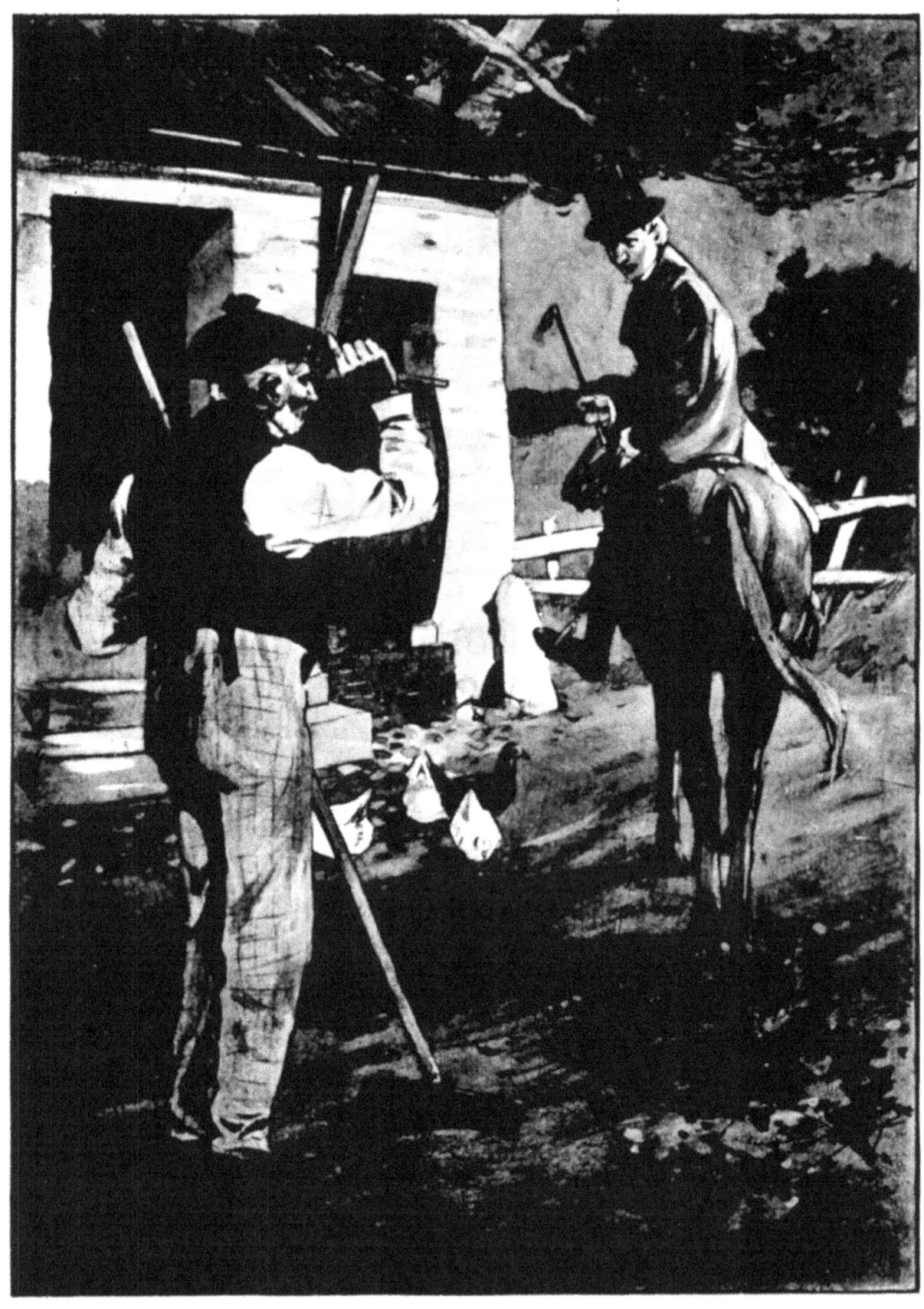

"I'm just speakin' to a man subject tae like passions wi' mysel'."— Page 10.

AUTOBIOGRAPHY OF PETER TAYLOR

PAISLEY: ALEXANDER GARDNER
Publisher by Appointment to the late Queen Victoria

1903

PRINTED BY
ALEXANDER GARDNER, PAISLEY

Dedicated

WITH EVERY FEELING OF RESPECT TO MY BRETHREN OF THE WORKING-CLASSES AND SPECIALLY TO THOSE WHO HAVE NEVER YET ENJOYED THE LUXURY OF PAYING THE . . . . INCOME TAX . . . .

PREFACE

HAVING often experienced a hunger for information about my own forbears, I began writing these *memoranda* for my own limited circle; but seeing their variety and extent, it has occurred to me they might be entertaining or helpful to others entering upon, or already in, the surging battle of life.

If I have made a mistake, it is a pity: I wish it was the first.

P. T.

CONTENTS

	PAGE
CHAPTER I	9

A Perthshire village in the "thirties"
—My kith and kin—Gregor M'Gregor

CHAPTER II - - - - - - 19

Paisley in 1840—A fight at the kirkyard gate—My schools and my schoolmasters

CHAPTER III - - - - - 38

I wish to be a sailor—My experiences in a brewery—Unfortunately I become chief bottler—"An engineer! oh name how sweet!"—Sawney and me—The man who "never saw mony hanged"—The dog "crib"

CHAPTER IV - - - - - - 55

To Blackwood & Gordon's—My chums —The grindstone club—"A fine

	PAGE

SCIENCE, GEOLOGY!"—THE NARROW ROAD—PAISLEY HARMONIC ASSOCIATION—I MEET MY WIFE—POEMS, SACRED AND SECULAR—PATE THE PRENTICE

CHAPTER V — 72

LOOKING FOR WORK—THE WORLD'S END—CHARLIE DICK—I DON'T GET ON WITH THE MANAGER—THAT BESOM, EVE—DUNDAS'S TOMB—VARIOUS MISFORTUNES AND TRIALS

CHAPTER VI — 94

KILMARNOCK—JACK SMITH—MY LANDLORD—DAN FRASER—HAMMERMAN'S STRIKE—AN ENGINE OFF THE LINE—FATHER AND SON—JAMIE CREE—THE CHRISTIAN ISRAELITES—TWO MISERS—JAMIE M'KIE—I GET SETTLED AND BECOME RESTLESS—PRAYER MEETINGS IN A TENEMENT

CHAPTER VII — 122

A DOWN-AT-THE-HEEL-MECHANIC—LIFE IN DERRY—NED FARREN AND HIS OWLD HORSE—I BECOME A SHAREHOLDER IN "THE SPURTLE"—THE FAMILY LIFE OF MR. ROSS, FOREMAN—HOW HE POPPED THE QUESTION

CONTENTS

	PAGE
CHAPTER VIII	137

OVER THE ALPS IN A DILIGENCE TO GENOA—SMUGGLED BOLTS—ANTONIO DANERE EX-ORGAN-GRINDER AND INTERPRETER—THE BURIAL OF THE SLATE—TAM M'GUIRE IN THE HOSPITAL—MR. WILTON—HOME AGAIN

CHAPTER IX	149

JOURNEY TO SICILY—LIFE IN THAT ISLAND—BRIGANDS—GARIBALDI—A LOYAL ORANGEMAN—A RELIGIOUS PROCESSION—A SICILIAN FUNERAL—REVOLVERS—A NOTED SCOUNDREL—HOME-COMING

CHAPTER X	166

OFF TO GALASHIELS—THE TRAVELLER'S REST—FREE LIBRARY—I BECOME A MEMBER OF THE SCHOOL BOARD—DEATH IN THE HOUSE—STEEL SPRINGS—THE HIGHLAND FLING—MY FIRST CHEQUE—A CO-PARTNERY—A CHILDREN'S CHURCH

CHAPTER XI	181

TWO LETTERS FROM CREWE

	PAGE
DIARY OF A TRIP TO AUSTRALIA	191

Bay of Biscay—Gibraltar—A death—Irish question—Lascars—Malta—Religion of to-day—Port Said—Suez—Aden—Fellow passengers—The Paisley Club—Colombo—Melbourne notes—Janolen caves—Rockymouth—Colonial diet—Victoria mint—Road home—Poetry—Egypt and the Pyramids—Malta—Discussions on sundry topics—Royalty and reminiscences

CONCLUSION	243

ILLUSTRATIONS

	PAGE
"I'm just speakin' to a man subject tae like passions wi' mysel'"	*frontispiece*
"Oh Peter, Peter, I pity your case"	12
"We fought for it"	21
A ministering angel .... *to face*	23
"Auld Bauldy"	24
The Hammils	31
"The Flowers o' the Forest"	35
"Oh yes, I'll give you a register-ticket"	41
The hider was discovered and I was on the market again	45
"To see me swagger doon the street"	47
"Sawney and me were at the kirk yesterday"	50
"Dae ye no see onything green?" .... *to face*	58
"A fine science, a fine science!" said Jamie	59
"Beside the chairman Vulcan sat"	69
The boys often went to the Broomielaw to see the steamer come home	75
"I never thought *you* would leave me"	78
He would plunge his big fist into his trouser pocket	81
"Is that no awfu'?"	86
I had to take the road again	93
Patrick Stirling	100
"Yourself made me a present of them trousers!" *to face*	102
The two Christian Israelites	109
Jamie, the miser	113
"I'll see you —— first"	116

	PAGE
The two paced up and down the yard	124
" Paddy is the cleverest man the Creator ever made "...	126
" Are ye going into that office, Mr. Taylor? "	128
Ned Farren and the " owld horse "	130
" Hae ye ony objection to mak' my parritch "	135
Antonio spoke English like a gentleman	140
They wended their way to the grave and buried the slate	143
" Four thirds for London," said I	151
His name was Baptiste	153
I bought a revolver	163
" The Traveller's Rest," Galashiels ....to face	168
Free Library, Galashiels...............to face	169
Charlie Dick ....to face	181
You would think one leg was six inches shorter than the other	193
" Biddy, Biddy, be a man and stan' "	206
" The Governor of Suez "	207
" What did you give for that? "	212
The Paisley Club	215
Janolen Caves ....to face	226
" There's that hanged thing staunin' ower there "	229
March 10th, 1863	240

Autobiography of Peter Taylor

CHAPTER I

A Perthshire village in the "thirties"—My kith and kin—Gregor M'Gregor

> "There's no a cottar wi' a ruif
> But bids ye welcome hither;
> There's no a farmer wi' a luif,
> But grips ye like a brither."
> —*Hugh Haliburton.*

I was born at Auchterarder Moor in 1837, on the 6th July, and am the sixth child of Peter Taylor and Janet M'Gregor. My father belonged to Blackford, and was the son of a crofter. His youth was spent in the little clachan of Bittergask. He had no sister and only one brother, known to us as "Uncle Willie." We heard so much of the latter at the winter fireside, and of the burn and braes of "Bithergarse," that I felt quite sure in my childish mind that the song of "Auld Lang Syne" was written in their honour, and that father and Uncle Willie were the very

> "Twa that ran aboot the braes
> And pu'd the gowans fine."

Willie was two years younger than father, and their mother died when Willie was a baby. My grandfather I do not remember, but my mother said he was a grand old man—tall, straight, and well-built—and full of the rugged independence characteristic of the Scottish race. He was at one time working on the Toll Roads, as they were called, and had the misfortune to have an altercation with the County Surveyor, a very haughty man, who demanded of grandfather, if he knew who he was speaking to. "Oo aye," said my grandfather, "I ken fine, Mr. Archer, I'm just speakin' to a man subject tae like passions wi' mysel'."

Life in Bittergask early in the nineteenth century, though falling short of many of the comforts of to-day, had many very pleasing features. Every woman could, and did, spin. The men could plough, build a farm steading, and many of them could weave.

My grandfather and his two sons were all masons. They had several acres of ground, kept a cow, and sometimes a horse. They went far and near in summer as masons, earning money to help to tide over the winter. The harvest was a time that took all the men and women possible into the fields, to cut, bind, and harvest the grain. Their winter fuel they cut, stacked, and dried from Shilforkie Moss. The children went to school every winter till they were almost men and women. My father was a well-educated man, and a very fair Latin scholar. Grandfather, having an idea common to the Scotch peasantry, wished to make him a minister; but the doctor who attended the family knocked that on the head by saying, " Ye may mak him a doctor, but a minister—never." And the medical man was right.

When there was a purpose of marriage between a young couple in the village, the male aspirant had to go and recover as many stones from the burn as would make the four walls of his house, and also look after clay for mortar. Then the whole of the villagers would turn out and give him a day's building, and by night they would have the walls ready for the roof—spars and thatch did the rest, and two box-beds made it into a but-and-a-ben. When the walls were finished, the villagers generally wound up with a dance in the barn, at which more engagements were entered into.

The little community could always furnish a

fiddler, a most important personage. The one who flourished in my father's day was a mason's labourer called Pate More. Pate " slade the stick out owre

"Oh Peter, Peter, I pity your case."

the string" with great art, and kept his instrument in a peculiar box like a spectacle-case. On one occasion the minister found him asleep in the early morning by the wayside, and the fiddle lying beside him. The minister shook him gently, and Pate opened his eye—he had but one. Said the minister, "Oh Peter, Peter, I pity your case;" and Peter replied, "Weel, minister, I dinna gie a —— for the case if the fiddle's hale."

Janet M'Gregor, my mother, belonged to Loch Tay side. Her father, like many another Highland fool, gave the best years of his life to his country for thirteen pence a day; and while he was fighting the nation's battles abroad, his wife and children were fighting their own at home. My mother was brought to Glasgow when she was twelve years old. After a time grandmother left her there in the house of an acquaintance while she herself went to the Curragh of Kildare to see her husband, whose regiment was there. But soon mother felt unhappy in the city, and longed for the Highland braes and the sight of her granny's face. Without more ado she started and footed it all the way to Loch Tay, which she reached after three days, being hospitably entertained every night by some good Samaritan. When the old clay biggin' appeared in view, all the pain and weariness were forgotten, and she made a rush for it, only to discover that it was turned into a stable, and no granny there. She was weeping bitterly, when a man entered and said—"Cheer up, your granny has flitted over to the other side of the loch, and the 'poat' will take you over in the morning."

My mother passed through Stirling on her way to Loch Tay on September 8th, 1820, the day Baird and Hardie were hanged for levying war against the King with eighteen pikes!

Mother was engaged to go to Bittergask to be servant-maid to Grandfather Taylor, and my own father was sent to bring her home. A thirty or forty mile tramp was common in those days—

> "Now what could artless Jenny do,
>   She hadna heart to say him na,
> At length she smiled a sweet consent,
>   And love was aye between them twa."

They were married on St. John's Eve, 1825, father being twenty-three years of age and mother nineteen.

My mother's aunt, Kate M'Gregor, did a thing which made every ear in the parish tingle, and every auld wife hold up her hands in horror: she consented to become the bride of Gregor M'Gregor, the poacher and smuggler. "All the king's horses and all the king's men" could not prevent the two from becoming man and wife. A gentleman, it was said, had left Gregor as a souvenir with a simple country girl, but it was so far to his credit that he helped to maintain the boy and pay for his education, which was greatly in excess of that given to the ordinary cottar's child. This extra accomplishment did not make Gregor a more law-abiding subject, but in fact no one at that time thought it a sin or a shame to smuggle whisky. Gregor was much mollified when I knew him, and his family, which consisted of three daughters, was grown up. I often listened to his stories, and I wish now that I had noted them in more detail. My mother was at his wedding, and Kate's party started from granny's door, headed by a piper; and when they got a mile on their way, they heard the strains of Gregor's piper coming with his party through the hills. The two processions met, and, headed by the two pipers, made for the manse; and there Gregor and Kate were united in the bonds of wedlock. People should not always be taken at their valuation in the public mouth. A better husband than Gregor never stepped in shoe-leather, so far as kindness and patience to his wife are concerned. To my certain knowledge, Kate was paralysed in her lower limbs for thirty years; but he never wearied of her; his love was as the love of Jonathan. I was often in his house, and know he coaxed, comforted, and fondled her as if she had been three years old. In my day Gregor had charge of the great water wheels at

Deanston Mills, and his three daughters worked there. The girls lifted the mother at breakfast time, made her snod, and left her seated in the armchair till they came back at two o'clock. It was the same in the afternoon till six in the evening. A neighbour might look in to see her, and many a time a daft man in the village would come up two or three steps of the stair and call aloud in Gaelic, " tatties and herrin'," to which she also replied in Gaelic; and these were almost all the incidents of the weary days. When I got Gregor on the crack, he would tell me something like this :—

" I remember one time we were coming to Stirling to sell a cart-load of whisky. We made a halt two miles out of the town, and I took a wee keg and went on in advance, going straight to the gauger's house before he would be out. When I saw him, I said, ' Mr. So-and-so, I have just come to see you, and here's a wee drap just for yersel', it wass very good, and how are you yersel', too?' And we would have a dram, and another dram; and we sat all day, and I entertained him, and the others sell't the whisky in Stirling. Sometimes our fellows drank more than was good for them, and had awful fights with the town's people. One night we were coming through a village, and there was a row; but in half-an-hour, no man would show his face outside the door. We were just leaving to go home, when I saw a man at a window. He thought he was safe because he was behind the glass. He pressed his nose and lips against it to make a fool of us, but a fellow of ours gave him one with his fist which knocked him to the middle of his own kitchen, glass and all. I lost a fine new coat wan day I was poaching in the wood. I had got some game, but was surprised to see a keeper coming over the fields; and when I looked, there was another and a dog. There was no doubt they wanted me, so I put myself in order. First, I took off my coat, for I did not want anything on they could hold on by. I hid it behind a bush, but never could find it again. I looked at the two men, and measured my distance to see if I could run between them before they could meet. I then took my gun, and started. I heard them cry to each other, but before they closed I was through. They hounded the dog after me, but I turned and cocked the gun. They whistled in an instant, and it was as well for the dog. I did not want to kill the brute; the keepers followed me no further, but I lost my good coat, yes, yes. I was up in the hills when I heard that Jenny was born, and I thought I would like to see her. So I took a wee keg, and started for home. Wha should I meet at Strathyre but the exciseman! 'It's a fine day, Gregor,' he said, 'that's the very keg I was looking for.' 'Well,' I says, 'I'm glad to get rid of it, for my shouther's sair.' I kent we were going the same road, so let him carry it till we were near the middle of the loch and the path dangerous. Then I catched him by the collar and said—'Lay down the whisky, lay down the whisky, will you; and if you say wan word or follow, I'll throw ye in the loch.' And we had a fine time when I went home to see wee Jenny."

Though there was the old fire still in his eye, he was a gentle soul. He emigrated with his girls long ago to America, leaving Kate behind, asleep among her native heather.

CHAPTER II

PAISLEY IN 1840—A FIGHT AT THE KIRKYARD GATE —MY SCHOOLS AND MY SCHOOLMASTERS

> " Whaur Cart rins rowin' to the sea
> By mony a flower and spreading tree."
> —*Burns.*

> " But human bodies are sic fools
> For a' their colleges and schools."
> —*Burns.*

IN 1839, our family removed to Paisley. Tam M'Gibbon of the Green Waa's farm drove them and their belongings to Stirling in his cart, from which by coach and boat we reached our destination. Tradition says I cried all the time on the coach, and sang " Sleeping Maggie " all the way on the boat.

It was the time of the great Railway Fever. My father was employed for a considerable time on the Joint Line between Paisley and Glasgow. I remember when he was an old man standing with him at the booking-office for Glasgow; looking at the old station-house, he said, "*I plumbed every stane in that wa'.*"

When the great collapse came, in the forties, there was great distress. Work could not be had, and men were going idle in thousands. Both fever and smallpox visited the family, and for a time it looked as if the hardy couple and their chicks were to be destroyed. A Mrs. Kinmont, who kept a shop in Williamsburgh, came in and said to mother—" Lassie, I'll send ye in a bow o' meal, and ye'll pay it when ye can." The meal was paid, but the debt of gratitude remains.

My sister Maggie died at No. 3 Williamsburgh in 1843. I was then six years of age. A sympathising neighbour called John Renfrew offered father a lair in the Gaelic kirkyard, where a baby had been buried the year previous. I remember Maggie's funeral well. I had no clothing to appear as a mourner on the solemn occasion, and mother was too overwhelmed with grief for the dead to think about the living, so I went to the funeral with the rest. It was my sister's, and I felt my importance among the other children. The coffin was carried on spokes by loving friends and sympathising neighbours, changing hands by the way to share the honour and also the burden. When we came to the gate, a boy, who I supposed was the gravedigger's son, refused

"We fought for it."

the accompanying children admission. I, being an interested party, challenged his right, and we fought for it. When to all appearance I was to be defeated, I called out lustily, " Father, father," and triumphed after all. I saw the coffin of my year-old sister, Jessie, lifted, and Maggie's lowered first and little Jessie's laid on the top. I have often thought on the lines of Mrs. Hemans—

> " They grew in beauty, side by side,
>   They filled one home with glee,
> Their graves are severed far and wide,
>   By mount, and stream, and sea."

But how often the children of the poor are separated, though they have died in the same town! Some of ours lie in the Gaelic churchyard, some in the East Relief, some in the West; father, mother, and one brother in the Paisley Cemetery, the latter being the only place where we have ground of our own. Thank God! there are many rich who do feel for, and help, the poor; but when all is said and done, the best to the poor are the poor themselves.

The first school I went to was an infant school in Lawn Street. My brother William, two years my senior, was my companion and guide. I remember stopping to look at a boy with a wooden gun, something like the old cross-bow, and watching the arrow fly. Willie went too near, and received it in his eye. This was a great calamity, and many a visit was made to the Glasgow Eye Infirmary. He grew

A ministering angel.—Page 23.

to be a good scholar, and was engaged as a clerk, but his health was undermined by the accident referred to, and he died in 1853, aged eighteen.

Two things I learned at the infant school which I have never forgotten. First, the advice which Joseph gave to his brethren—" See that ye fall not out by the way ;" and second—" Pure religion and undefiled before God and the Father is this, to visit the fatherless and the widows in their affliction, and to keep yourselves unspotted from the world "—a chart well-fitted to take gentle and simple through the mazes of human life with pleasure and profit.

By and by the family removed to Thread Street, in order that my father might be nearer his work in the Brewery, where he started at 12s. per week, and was afterwards promoted to be gaffer at the ransom of 15s. The hours generally were from four in the morning till six at night, five days a week, the sixth being from six A.M. till six P.M.; he had to go back twice on Sunday to turn the malt. And yet it took great influence to get him into this work, for which we had to thank the Misses Brown of Crossflat, especially Miss Elizabeth, who was a ministering angel, and waited on my sister Maggie, getting from her divine consolation as well as giving it. My poor mother, who lacked that full assurance so comforting to many, never for a moment, after Maggie's death, doubted that she was the mother of children in heaven.

The Seedhill School, to which I was next transferred, was a queer place, and so was the dominie, called by us naughty boys, "Auld Bauldy." He had only one hand, and it would have been a mercy for us if he had had two. His left hand was off at the wrist, and the stump was the terror of our lives; you never knew till it landed in your neck, and the coruscations that danced before your eyes were bewildering. The writing was all done with quills, though steel pens were in the market. It was quite a sight to see us all standing round the desk waiting to have our quills mended, imagining that if we could only get a good pen we would be splendid writers. Then we had copy-lines on slips of

"Auld Bauldy."

cardboard as old as himself and the colour of an orange. When he lifted the bundle to give them out, you never heard such a babel; several cried: "roon write," another batch: "sma' write," a third: "sma' write, twa lines," and a fourth kept pegging away at "half-text." The school was what is known in Paisley as a six-loom shop, that is, at one time it held six weavers. During the racket alluded to, the other classes were supposed to be getting on with their own special work, but of their progress I cannot speak.

Then we never did any sums in subtraction in that school; when we finished addition, we were put into "from-take." Our slates declared it and we believed it. It was a matter of honour how philosophically we could take the loofies, and many a time I held the unruly member between my teeth to keep it quiet, when it would have been a luxury to cry. I fought sundry battles at this school with varying success; my mother once told me that I had had more black e'en than all her other sons put together. I do not think that I was a quarrelsome boy, but I would not submit to any injustice or stand by and see another wronged. I remember quite a party of us starting for a "soom" at Bauldy's Brig in the Canal. There was a boy with us called

Andrew Morrison—poor fellow, he was hardly up to the standard, mentally or physically, and was called "Goosie." He was badly treated that day by a boy, Sawnie Knox, who latterly cut Morrison's heel with a stone. I remonstrated, with the result that Sawnie Knox and myself were rolling in the Seedhill Road in less than two minutes. We fought a long time and I was badly punished, for he was a "fister." At the end of one round he was lying on the top of me; and as he held me by the neck, he said, "Are ye no bate yet?" and I replied, "If ye let me up, I'll tell ye." When we got up Sawnie said he wasna gaun to fecht ony mair. These were the sweetest words I had heard that day. I never taunted him; I was too glad; and the boys accorded me the victory, an honour I carried with great humility.

Some parents are in an awful stew if their boys have an occasional fight. I hardly ever knew of a boy that was not the better of a thrashing once in a while; and none can do it with more effect than his own school chums. It teaches him the same lesson the Apostle teaches men: "not to think of himself more highly than he ought to think, but to think soberly."

I remember a real gala-day at that school. It was the season of foot-races which always came to white-heat about St. James' Day Fair. Our race-course was the back-road called Mill Street, from the old granary on the top to the foot of the brae at the entrance to Kilnside House, at that time belonging to Whitehead of the tan-works. All our jackets, vests, bonnets, books and slates, were deposited on the grass-plots at the entrance, and this was an offence to Whitehead's people. Some men came out of the policies and scooped the whole show, took them inside and shut the gate. We clamoured loud and long for our property, till a messenger arrived who told us it was all in the school, and Mr. Muir was waiting for us. We formed into solemn and grotesque procession, and marched to our doom. There were no lessons that day, at least of the ordinary kind. It was like a jumble sale. The master stood, armed with the tawse; a jacket was held up: "Whose is this?" it had to be redeemed. The fact is, most of us had to claim three or four times. It took the whole forenoon to adjust matters, and the school that day was like Rama of old—lamentation, and weeping, and great mourning.

I often think there has been a great contrast between my early and my later years. Misfortune dogged my boyhood, and success my later life. I was especially unlucky in the matter of breaking windows, which my parents could ill afford to pay. The climax came one day when the Seedhill School had a stone battle with Thread Street School. We fairly routed the latter, and chased them into their play-ground. Some of us climbed the wall in Mill Street, which overlooked the grounds, and hurled defiance at them, little thinking that there was some one taking notes. I had scarcely got home, when two policemen came to the door and asked if this was where Peter Taylor stayed.

My mother said "Yes; was it the boy or the faither?"

"Oh! the boy."

Then there was a great sob and cry. "What has he been daein' noo?"

The heart of the law was touched, and one of them laid a kind hand on her shoulder and said, "Don't cry, my good woman; we are only come to frighten him."

Good old bobby! He comforted me more than my mother that day. The ringleaders, of whom I was one, had to pay 1s. 6d. each, and the other scholars a penny, which considerably dimmed the victory of yesterday.

There was another old custom in full swing at the

school, in which I never had the pleasure of sharing. It was held at Candlemas; the scholars all brought the master presents. Life was so hard and bare at Thread Street, that to contribute, however willing, was quite out of the question. The master had sweets and cakes, etc., for the scholars, and the tawse had a holiday. The scholars who gave the most valuable gift, were king and queen for the time being. One year, I specially remember, the queen gave the master half-a-crown; this was considered by us magnificent. Poor old Mr. Muir, I have no doubt he needed all he got, for fees were small. There was an old woman (I am sorry I forget her name) who lived but-and-ben with the school. She was a great friend to the boys; she always met us at the door and took our dirty shinties when these were in vogue, and sometimes when we were late, or in other troubles, she would even go in and speak for us, a very courageous thing to do in our estimation. Then there was Mirren Semple's next door, where we parted with our old copy-books for a bit of "blackman," and then came the joy of a new copy. What resolutions we made to keep it clean, and write our very best copperplate, and make it a credit to us; just as in later life, we have begun a new year with strong determination to play the man more than in any of the preceding, but as it advanced, what with carelessness and mishaps, we lost heart as we did with the copy—perfection being very far away!

Few people would believe what a village was in Seedhill at that time, on the ground now covered by the gigantic thread works of Messrs. Clark.

What a number of thriving families and curious old-fashioned people there were! There was an old weaver called Johnnie Robin, a favourite with the boys, a bit of a Nimrod in his way, though we never saw any of his hunting; but we have seen him net the Linn below the Hammils, and shake trout out of it more than once. He was also fond of animals, and we used to get great fun with a monkey he kept. That creature gave us any amount of chat when we paid him a visit. He was tethered to the door of the close where Johnnie lived. We had a trick of getting behind our neighbour, and pushing the latter within the sentinel's sphere of influence, and our long-tailed ancestor left his mark on a lot of us.

We sometimes went to the tan-works for lime, and limed the "mill holes," as we called them—that was when the wheels were stopped—and flounders and eels came out in abundance. Swimming was a great feature in summer weather. The boys learned in the mill lade, Seedhill side, above the Hammils, and when sufficient proficiency was attained, they went to the deeper waters below. It was no unusual thing to see scores of boys and men on the rocks, and no boy was considered a swimmer till he could

The Hammils.

jump the Hammils and tail the Linn—when he had passed over the "Plumb" or deep part, he stood and folded his arms to shew the deed was done. Many of my young mates were drowned there. It was an anxious time for parents. Indeed, what with bathing in summer and sliding in winter, there was no cessation of anxiety. What a mercy we now have swimming-ponds and skating-ponds, where the young can enjoy themselves in safety!

Mr. John Harran, a tanner, who lived close by, saved about thirty-nine lives (if my memory is good), and received a public testimonial. Talk of "The March of the Cameron Men," you should have heard the tramp of clogs as the tanners ran with their long poles at the double, when the cry of a drowning reached them. Harran went straight into the water without divesting himself of anything save his clogs, which he did, as he ran, hopping first on one foot and then on the other. You could see his Glengarry bonnet heading straight for the place where the unfortunate had gone down. Good old soul, he saved many a one's child, but could not save his own, who was drowned in one of the tan pits.

There was one day in the year at Mr. Muir's school that had great attraction for us: it was called Recitation Day. We were very ambitious as to the part we might get. My joy knew no bounds one year, when I was assigned the favourite piece, "Cato's Soliloquy on the Immortality of the Soul." The charm of this piece lay in the fact that it required a dagger, and the master had one for the purpose. I was all in a flutter when I was called. Stepping boldly forth, and stretching out the hand like the

Apostle of the Gentiles, I cried, "It must be so, Plato."

"Tut, tut, tut," said the maister, "it must not be so, Peter. Sit down, man, sit down," and he brought me an old Bible, and said it was to be the works of Plato. I was to be absorbed in the works of the philosopher, and, finally becoming convinced of the truth of his arguments, to exclaim, "It must be so," etc.

But, alas, the fire was out. What heart had I to declaim about the wreck of matter and the crash of worlds? I smiled sickly at the drawn dagger and defied its point, and was glad when it was over, convinced that whatever I was good for, it was not Cato.

By and by I was transferred to Thread Street School, to a teacher called Mr. Hosie, a very austere man, but one who had a good reputation for teaching. He certainly deserved a good one for thrashing, though he never punished me extremely. He had a queer custom of always awarding the writing prize to No. 5 and not to No. 1. This seemed strange, but it was the case, and no doubt he had his reasons. I remember an old Highland cowfeeder who came to the school more than once to urge the master not to spare the rod on *his* boys, and the master did not. Query: Did it do any good?

I do not think so. The boys in turn punished others as they had been punished themselves, and were for years the terror of the youngsters in the New Toon. I remember working with one of the sons in the south of Scotland when we were both about thirty years of age, and one Sunday we had a long crack about old times.

"Man, Peter," he said, "I often think my faither dealt very strangely with us when we were children. We were a' born in Paisley; nevertheless, we had to gang to the Gaelic Kirk every Sunday. What did we ken aboot Gaelic? Not only that, but we had to take hands and to make two and two in procession, my faither and mother bringing up the rear. We could hear the windows go flying up, and see the folk running to the doors, crying, 'Here they're coming! Come and see the Flowers o' the Forest.'"

I am no believer in extreme punishment, and in this case it was a failure. The fewer cast-iron laws in a household the better; the children learn more from what they see you do than from what they hear you say in the way of precept. And mercy is twice blessed.

A boy played truant one day, and the master was determined to have it out with him. The lad's mother used to wash the schoolroom floor, and some

"The Flowers o' the Forest."

thought he paid no fees. I cannot say for the truth of the report, but it was evident that day that the master was preparing for a big flogging. We were all drawn up in a semi-circle; and the lad, seeing what was coming, made a dash for the door, and escaped. Four of the biggest lads were at once despatched to bring him back. In about ten minutes I was sent off to tell the four never to mind, but to come back themselves. I could see no one when I started, but I took the Glasgow Road, enquiring every little bit, " Did you see four fellows running forward there?" " Yes, they are a little bit ahead." I ran, and rested and ran again till I reached Ibrox (I know it now by the railway crossing the road). I was not inclined to go any further, and returned home faint and weary; it was after 4 P.M., and the school was over for the day. The four others brought back the culprit about six o'clock, but the master dismissed them till the following day. That next day was one to be remembered. The door was locked. First, the master thrashed the boy till he was tired, and then told him to ask the school's pardon for what he had done the day before. In days when manners were different from what they are now, that was a serious humiliation, and the boy refused. A punishment followed which deserved penal servitude. The boy was caned up and down, back and fore, head, body, legs, and feet. If anybody had shot that master, I would have cried "Bravo." The boy and the master were both alike stubborn. A boy I knew once played truant in order to go to Glasgow to see the "Lords" come in. His master next day made *him*, for a punishment, give the whole school a description of all he had seen. The laughter which was provoked by his humiliation did every one good; and the teacher earned the everlasting esteem and regard of the delinquent. Mr. Hosie was not without his good points, and used to encourage us to learn off our catechism by giving a penny to the most proficient.

CHAPTER III

I WISH TO BE A SAILOR—MY EXPERIENCES IN A BREWERY—UNFORTUNATELY I BECOME CHIEF BOTTLER—"AN ENGINEER! OH NAME HOW SWEET!"—SAWNEY AND ME—THE MAN WHO "NEVER SAW MONY HANGED"—THE DOG "CRIB"

> "Labour
> Knocks with her hundred hands at the golden gates of the morning."
> —*Longfellow.*

> "Blest work! if ever thou wert curse of God,
> What must his blessing be!"
> —*J. B. Selkirk.*

By the time I was eleven-and-a-half years of age, my brother Willie, who was message-boy in a shop, turned ill, and I was sent to take his place. My brother's illness was long, so the master said he would just keep me. The master was a queer fish, very strict in some things and very loose in others. Several quaint characters came about the shop. One was a Mr. Carlile, of a good family and well up in years, who was boarded in Paisley. His daily walk was from Gateside, where he lived, to the Cemetery and home again. He had two ports of call which he took both on the outward and the inward voyage —the Police Office and our shop. He was a little bit off mentally, and the boys in the street called him "Snuffy Geordie." He would answer to no name but Mr. Carlile. When my master was in the humour, he would say to me: "Here's Mr. Carlile coming; let us have some fun." He would then take his pipe, sit down in the back-shop and cry: "Come away, Mr. Carlile." I would also bid the latter good morning with great politeness, and the moment he had passed I would draw my breath with violence through my nostrils, at which he would start and turn round at once. The master would say: "Would you stand that, Mr. Carlile?" Then back he would come to see if I was the offender, and pretend to box my ear, but such a gentle touch as he had! My conscience smites me as I think of it. He would proceed once more to the back-shop, assured I was still his friend. He would be comfortably seated and his snuff-box out, when another sniff from me would bring him to his feet like an earthquake. Sometimes I had to jump the counter to escape him.

Besides making fun to order, I made some that was not wanted. Altogether, my first place was a failure. The master complained of me often, and as my elder brother was in the shop, it was a heartbreak to him. The thing came to a speedy end as follows. I was sent out a message one morning, and after that, was to be free to go for breakfast. Before returning to the shop, I met a boy whose father was a schoolmaster and a naturalist. The boy somehow asked me into his home, and showed me his father's collection of butterflies and insects, which was marvellous and beautiful. It was ten o'clock before I knew where I was. I had not been home, and, as I was always a little better dressed after breakfast, I could not return to the shop as I was. I met another boy and told him the situation, and we both resolved to go to sea. So to Glasgow we set off for a ship. Whilst my chum and I were discussing, I saw my mother dressed in her best hurrying to the shop. I knew it was on my account. What a blessing it would have been if I had spoken to her! and what remorse it would have saved me! But no, I hid in a close till she passed.

We found it much more difficult to get a ship than we had anticipated. We simply spoke to Tom, Dick, and Harry, lumpers and quay-porters. One man said, "If you want a ship, go to the Shipping Office." Accordingly we went there; I did all the speaking. A person asked us, "Have you a register-ticket?" Never having heard of such a

"Oh yes, I'll give you a register-ticket."

thing, we inquired for the register office and went in. I said to the gentleman in charge: "We are anxious to go to sea; would you please give us a register-ticket?" He took a good long look at us and said: "Oh yes, I'll give you a register-ticket." He walked over to a desk, lifted a ruler, and made a dash at us, and in the twinkling of half an eye, as Mansie Waugh says, we were both in the middle of the street. The situation was becoming desperate; the day was far gone; and we were weary. We each purchased half-tickets to Stirling. I had an aunt at Deanston, seven miles beyond, and that was the only haven of rest I could think of. I have learned since, that the day after, father and mother searched the Glasgow shipping for me, and later on, that of Greenock as well. When I think of it, God have mercy on me, for the old folk forgave me long ago! My mother overtook me at Deanston, sent the other boy home, saying it was not every day she was there, and would stay a day or two. I came home with her, crest-fallen indeed. There was still my father to face, and I was wicked enough to resolve that if he thrashed me, he would not have the chance of doing so for a long time again. When it came near the dinner-hour, I made an excuse to go out. But such a plan could not continue; I had to face him at six o'clock. I was sitting looking steadfastly at the fire when he came in. He simply said: "Well, Pate, I'm glad to see ye back." My sailor days were at an end.

I was sent to school again till something would

turn up. My father at length got me a job in the brewery. It was a most unsuitable place for me, for, though I was bad enough, I met some there who could give me points. No doubt I enjoyed the place. I remember there was a boy who had cast out with his parents, and who said he was going home no more, but would sleep in the hay-loft above the stable. By dinner-time he had two or three disciples who were going to sleep with him. One of these was my special chum, Sawnie Gordon; this set up my ambition, so I asked mother as a great favour to be allowed to sleep that night with Sawnie, and got permission. Talk of bogles and ghosts and mahatmas! There were scenes in the brewery that night that might have scared anybody. We found it more difficult to sleep among hay than we had anticipated, so we rose and wandered about the whole place, and spent an hour or two beside the chaffer that heated the kiln for roasting the malt. There we sat near midnight, in the lurid light, like Macbeth's witches. The sight of us would have startled Banquo or any other stranger. If we had fallen asleep beside that charcoal fire I don't think we should have awakened again, and it would have been no great loss except to ourselves and to those whose love for us was inextinguishable. But the sulphur was too strong for us, and we went back to the stable. After we were in the loft a carter came in late, stabled and fed his horse, and went home, little thinking there were embodied spirits in the vicinity. We duly appeared at our work at six A.M. The men at once discovered from the hayseeds and from our general appearance where we had spent the night.

On one occasion I was promoted to be chief bottler. If my memory serves me right, we could bottle 300 dozen a day. Very likely I was anxious to understand my business thoroughly, as well as become also a good judge of the quality of the beer. So when the manager came in about night-fall I was quite open to give him some advice how to manage his business. He said he would consider my proposals next day. He did consider them on the morrow: he sent for me and talked to me like a father, telling me among other things that I was a disgrace to his work. I have been trying to make amends for my conduct ever since, and, strange to say, the brewers are not pleased with me yet! We had been bottling sweet ale for the master's own house. Now, the boys liked the sweet but not the bitter. So we drew cuts who should hide a bottle for further use, and the lot fell on Jonah. The bottle was hidden and the hider discovered, and I was on the market again.

My old brother, James, got me a job as an apprentice mechanic. Perhaps I should say a word

The hider was discovered and I was on the market again.

here about James. A more exemplary son never lived. He was seven years older than myself, and a great comfort to my mother. We all thought him a great man when he had saved £70. When he went his summer holidays he would always have mother down for three or four days, usually to Largs. His principal companion was brother Willie, and when the latter died, James fastened on to me. He died at the age of twenty-eight, having been married about six months, and left a widow but no issue. I believe his death was the severest blow the old folks ever got; they were just getting out of the wood, and Jim was the pioneer. "God moves in a mysterious way." Well, James got me in as an apprentice mechanic, and said, "If you don't behave this time, I'll never speak for you again."

I started with Mr. Robert Kerr, shawl manufacturer, who kept a good staff of mechanics. I versified my start some years afterwards as follows:—

1854.

> The new-born year scarce showed her head,
> When I set aff to learn a trade;
> To see me swagger doon the street,
> An engineer (oh name how sweet!)
> I met my auld chums gaun to schule,
> Nor tried to hide my twa-foot rule,
> Wi' big brass joint twa inch abune
> The moleskin pouch I held it in.
> And when the smith rang on the studdie,
> Up han' or ower hip I was ready,
> I blew the bellows, like to burst,

"AN ENGINEER!"

And burnt the heat, got kicked and curst;
I scaled the wa's and ran for grog,
And screwed the bolts and fed the dog.
Thus passed year first in humble station,
Wark wasna wark—but recreation.

"To see me swagger doon the street."

From the blowing of the smith's bellows and the screwing of bolts, I was promoted to the turning-lathe. I must say I took great interest in this work, even when I was merely blowing the bellows or giving the smith a chap. I used to go in during the meal-hours and stick any quantity of double flooring nails in a wooden block, and then swinging the fore-hammer " ower hip," as it was called, knock them in one by one. It cost the master something for nails, and if he did not get repaid by increased proficiency, then I am in his debt. It takes longer to become a good striker than some imagine. One day I was not pleasing the old smith in the way I was putting down the hammer, so he stopped abruptly and, looking at me, he said wrathfully, " Dae ye think it's razors ye're makkin'? "

I remember receiving a rebuke from that smith that did me good all the days of my life, and which shows the necessity of men taking a little interest in the boys committed to their care. One of the mechanics who came to get his tools dressed at the smithy fire, was always full of questionable stories. I did not comprehend their full import at the time, but anything with a comic element in it was sure to set me off in a roar.

The smith was one day speaking to another of the men about this fellow and his stories, when he turned sharp upon me and said, " And you are no better, or you wadna laugh at him as you do."

Thanks, Willie, for that rebuke; I mind it still, and reverence you for it.

I was put to work with a nice old man, indeed, I should say old *gentleman*. He was much more refined than the ordinary stock. His name was Alexander Watt. He had seen better days, and was at one time manager of a large cotton mill in the neighbourhood of Paisley, but had to fall back on his trade in his declining years. He was so far unfortunate, poor fellow, as to have a very conspicuous nose, and was rather sensitive about it. He had only one son, and the love between them was very strong, but he would not go to live with the son as long as he was able to maintain himself. " I would be a bonnie like dearie," he would say to me, " hurling a perambulator." He was the first one to teach me decimals; he taught me also to calculate speeds, driven by belt-pulleys or gearing. He also lectured me on the steam engine more than I could comprehend. When I left Mr. Kerr's, he succeeded in getting me into a marine shop to finish my time. Many a happy, happy day old Sandy and I had together. He was very lonely, and his love fell upon me. I could use great familiarity with him, without giving any offence. He always spoke of himself as a dual being—Sawney an' he, or, Sawney and me, were at the kirk yesterday; Sawney and he cast out, etc.

"Good morning," I would say to him, "I hope I see you well, Mr. Watt."

"Thank thee, Pate," he would reply; "I'm gae weel mysel', but Sawney's gieing me some trouble."

"Oh, I think you're ower sair on Sawney. What's he been daein' noo?"

"Thou sees, Pate, when my wife was livin', she could manage him fine; noo there's naebody to look after him but me, and he disna care so much for me. Weel, we gaed up the toon for a walk last nicht, and wha should we meet, but an auld freen we hadna seen for years, and naething wad dae us but a dram. Man, Sawney was happy. I wanted him to rise and come away at ten o'clock, but not he. So, we sat later, and then at the bell this morning he wadna rise, and pled for a sleep till

"Sawney and me were at the kirk yesterday.

breakfast time. My certes! I gied him a rare thrashing, and made him rise."

A few years after, I entirely lost sight of my old friend. There is no more pitiable object than the aged tradesman with vigour and sight failing, the demand being for the young. Fellows of twenty-two will grow all the hair on their face possible, to make them look manly, and at fifty they will shave all off, to hide grey hairs and make them look young. Sandy never said a word to me I would wish unsaid, and if we meet again in the long hereafter, there will be nothing but pleasant memories between us.

There was another old fellow in that shop I did not get on so well with. I could not make him out: he was either up in the third heavens with joy, or down in the dungeon with sorrow. The pay-day, which was the happiest in all the fortnight to me, was always the dullest with him. I reasoned out the wherefore long afterwards, but at the time it was passing strange. He was connected with the master by marriage, and was a sort of pensioner. When he was in a good key, however, I could get him to relate the same experiences over and over again. I had to take a certain line of introduction, and then simply say, "Johnnie, did you ever see onybody hanged?"

He would put down the point of his file on the

bench at once, and resting on the handle, say, "I never saw mony."

Then he would tell us how, when he was working with so-and-so, the gunsmith in Glasgow, the latter came in one morning and said, " You fellows had better gang awa' doon and see thae three men hanged this mornin', and see if it'll no mak' ye behave yoursel's. It was a terrible crush, and we saw the men brocht on, and the rapes put roon their necks, and the white nichtcaps drawn ower their faces. And the yin that had the napkin in his haun wadna gie the signal, till I saw the hangman gang up and speak tae him."

Then would follow the history of some more that were hanged for sheep-stealing, and of men and women sent to their long account for theft and other petty crimes. We counted that Johnnie had seen about a dozen hanged; but he aye maintained that *he never saw mony.* Although I could get the sunny side of Johnnie for a blink, as a rule he looked at me askance. I overhead the men discussing me one day, when they were not aware that I was listening, and Johnnie's opinion was that I was a clever boy, but a —— sight too clever, an opinion I could not understand.

There was a dog in that place, already referred to

in the rhyme. As it was my duty to feed him till a younger boy arrived, he had a decided preference for me, and accompanied me home at all the meal-times. I used to make him ashamed when I offered him a half-quarter loaf: he knew I was making a fool of him, and did not like it. His name was "Crib," a black-and-tan—a demon to fight, and scarred all over the head. That dog knew nine A.M., two P.M., and six in the evening as well as any man in the shop. I have seen us lift our coats and put them on at eight A.M., as if it was breakfast-time; but you could not awaken any enthusiasm in Crib till nine A.M., and then you could not repress it. Before six in the evening he decamped, and I hunted the weavers' shops for him, and brought him back in disgrace to be chained for the night. He gave no quarter to cats or rag-pickers; he simply tore the bag off the backs of the latter, and they dared not touch it till some of the men relieved them. Poor old brute! he got so old and infirm that it was resolved to drown him. I could not take a hand at that job, but I saw the procession start. The dog was much liked by the men; and, in fun, I suppose, they offered five shillings reward for the best poem on him. I blame this for setting me on to rhyme. I got the first prize, but not the five shillings, and so am no mercenary. I can remember only two verses—

>Noo cats wi' joy can loup and spring
> And wander to and fro,
>And midden mavises* may sing
> The death of Crib, their foe.
>
>But nae joy sparkles in our een,
> We mourn thy loss richt sair,
>Adieu, adieu, my sonsie freen,
> We'll never see thee mair!

* Paisley name for rag-picker.

CHAPTER IV

I GO TO BLACKWOOD & GORDON'S—MY CHUMS—THE GRINDSTONE CLUB—"A FINE SCIENCE, GEOLOGY!"—THE NARROW ROAD—PAISLEY HARMONIC ASSOCIATION—I MEET MY WIFE—POEMS, SACRED AND SECULAR—PATE THE PRENTICE

> " At times the thing is balanced sae,
>   O joy ye hae a junk;
> An' neest your very hert is wae,
>   For Life's a hedderkin-dunk."
> —*Rasmie's Büddie.*

I SERVED three years and two months with Mr. Robert Kerr, and then went to Messrs. Blackwood & Gordon, shipbuilders and engineers, my testimonials showing that in my first place as a mechanic I had "given satisfaction in attention and attendance." Have patience, O ye mothers, who are yearning for a glowing report of your boys! I was informed that, as I had not been where I could learn as much as if I had been with Messrs. Blackwood & Gordon, I would have to lose a year—that is, I had to serve them for other three years, wages being six, seven, and eight shillings a week. The term seemed long; but, as I had no alternative, I accepted, hoping to make up for lost time in the future. I saw such fine work in this place that my joy was intense. The first job I got was to bush some links, cut out the cotter holes, and finish them. You bet when that engine was started, I made an excuse to go on board; and, as I looked at the play of the magnificent machine, I said to myself, "You have helped to make that engine at anyrate." I looked at it long and lovingly, watching the advance and retreat of the various parts, but I always came back to the links, for no part of it had the same interest for me as the part I had made myself.

We had all sorts and conditions of men in this place—quiet men and noisy men, sober and the reverse, good and bad mixtie-maxtie; also a great deal of young blood—over fifty apprentices, some of them very intelligent lads. My principal chums were Sandy M'Lean from Largs and Bob Crawford from Kilbirnie, the former nick-named "Hielan' Sawney," and the latter "Pie Willie." When a new boy came to the work he had to stand a good deal of banter, the wise (?) ones doing everything in their power to lead him astray while pretending to give him information, their real purpose being to make him a laughing-stock. M'Lean started soon after his arrival to make a pocket-square, and was busy at it every meal-hour. One day he was sawing away at the stock which was to receive the blade, and, poor chap, he was making little progress, the saw being very blunt. One fellow said, " Put some red lead on it if you want it to cut." Sandy at once proceeded to do this, while the other went round and called the men to come and have a look. A great burst of laughter convinced Sandy that it was folly to put trust in princes or men's sons. By and by, the wee hielandman had it out with the same wag. The latter was very proud of his skill in taking what are termed fires out of people's eyes—*i.e.*, small specks of metal. He was lecturing M'Lean one day in the presence of some others, and putting him through the process vulgarly called "swelling his head." But once bitten twice shy; Sandy felt he was being made a fool of, and while showing great interest, began rubbing one eye.

The orator at once said, " Is there something in your e'e?"

Sandy did not think there was much wrong, but the oculist insisted on having a look, and look he did up and down. A crowd was waiting for the verdict, but the doctor declared he could not see a thing.

Says Sandy, "Dae ye no see onything green?" and a roar of laughter followed, as the magnetised knife was restored to its scabbard.

THE GRINDSTONE CLUB.—A number of the lads who were fond of discussion, and of hearing anything new, like the men of Athens, used to converge on one of the grindstones every day about twelve noon, when the gaffer went for his smoke. The grindstone we preferred was one commanding a view of the stair, where we could see the approach of anyone in authority, and quickly radiate to our several lathes and benches. Eye-service, you will say; yes, and it bothered my conscience at times. Great topics were discussed there, and one old infidel, called James Blair, required that grindstone at twelve noon as much as any of us. Jamie was a joiner to trade, but was too old for a regular hand, and was at this time kept principally for shafting hammers. He sometimes spent the winter in the Paisley Poorhouse, but made a "fend" outside in summer. I asked him one day how he liked the Poorhouse.

"Fairly, fairly," was the reply; "spiritual food abundant; temporal —— thin."

"Dae ye no see onything green?"—Page 58.

He was a well-informed man, and conversant with many things, but his hatred to religion, and to everything we had been taught to revere, made him feared. He turned his old haggard face on us one day, and said:

"Wouldn't I be a bonnie-like beauty, sittin' in Heaven singin' hallelujahs till I was hairse."

I mind him coming to the club and saying:

"Well, lads, what's the topic the day?"

Some one answered, "We're speaking about geology."

"A fine science, a fine science!" said Jamie.

"A fine science, a fine science!" said Jamie. "What's this that fellow Paul says?—'By one man sin entered into the world, and death by sin, and so death passed upon all men.' Rank nonsense! Read Hugh Miller and he'll shew you death was in the world before there was a man to sin."

That was a crusher, and Jamie gave one of his occasional smiles which revealed both of his teeth, and departed, leaving his argument to simmer. Jamie made remarks I would not write. If his faith has not done more for him where he has gone than it did here, then it was a great failure.

M'Lean, Crawford, and I agreed to have a school one winter to improve our time; we met in our house, mother agreeing to give us the kitchen. We met three nights a week and practised arithmetic. By and by we resolved to form a Mutual Improvement Association, confined to the 'prentices of the shop. In a short time we had a score of members. One young journeyman asked to be admitted, and, as he was quite as young as some of ourselves, we made an exception in his case. His name was Alexander Forrest.* He still lives at Stockport. I have not as yet seen him since those days, but we have discovered each other and exchanged letters and photos. Mr. Forrest has twice contested South Salford in the Liberal interest, but unsuccessfully; let us hope that the third time will be lucky. In one of his recent letters to me he said: "Comfort-

---

* Mr. Forrest, who once read in my house the above passage in my diary, has now, I regret to say, passed over to the majority.

able in my business and happy in my home, what more could a fellow desire?"

One of the rules of our Association was: "Meetings shall be opened and closed with prayer." Didn't that give rise to a lot of chaff in Blackwood & Gordon's. Notwithstanding, we stuck to our guns, and profane swearing went down 50 per cent.

Going back to my work one breakfast hour, I took up a position at the outside of a great crowd that had gathered at the gate, in order to hear what was going on. Some one cried, "How did ye get on, Cobbler? Tell us a' about it."

The Cobbler was a great comic. His father was a shoe-maker, so you can understand the nick-name.

"Weel," says the Cobbler, "the meeting was opened wi' prayer, of course, and then Peter Parley began his essay. His subject was 'Broad is the way that leadeth to destruction and many there be which go in thereat, while narrow is the way,' etc. Weel, d'ye ken, Peter made a grand job o't. He warned the meetin' to be carefu', for there was a nasty bias in the best o' us for the braid road; for instance, says he, suppose this room was on fire: nae doot the maist o' ye wad mak' for the door, while only ane or twa o' ye wad mind the narrow road and *gang up the lum*."

Then the black beggars exploded with laughter, in which we no doubt joined, but with the blood mantling in our cheeks. But they laugh best who laugh last. Peter Parley, who never gave an essay on any such subject, declared his principles in his youth, maintained them in his manhood, and, after a long, useful, and honoured life, is now retired and living in our neighbourhood, crowning a youth of labour with an age of ease, while the poor Cobbler and many others who made merry at his expense, have passed into the great unseen without any apparent elevation in one sense or another.

I might here pause to speak of another meeting which some of us organised to amuse ourselves on the winter Saturday evenings. These hung very heavy on our hands; in those days there were no Saturday evening concerts, and, even if there had been, we had no money to pay for them. So we had to provide something cheap. We took a schoolroom, for which we paid 1s. 6d. a night, gas included. We called our society, "The Paisley Harmonic Association." Some of our members knew a little of music. We bought some of Cameron's sacred music books, and sang from them on the Saturday evenings from eight till nine, and from nine till ten we had songs and recitations. The lads paid $1\frac{1}{2}$d. each, and the girls were admitted free. The success which attended these meetings, so far as giving pleasure to the young folks, was quite phenomenal, and we often used to see the lassies home. I wrote several rhymes for the annual social meeting of this association: one of them was called "Our Last May Spree." I wrote another entitled "A Dream," which was recited by our chairman, Mr. Hugh Kerr, now a photographic artist. I have a copy of this poem, which was a kind of Tam o' Shanter piece, and introduced a good number of our own chums and other characters I would have been better to have left alone.

One night I met a girl who attended our meetings, and I stopped to talk to her. She stole before my eyes my very best silk handkerchief, a "hanky" kept entirely for show, and beautifully adjusted to look modestly out of my pocket. This complimentary theft was committed, as you may suppose, on a Sunday night, for that handkerchief was never abroad on any secular occasion. As the girl refused to give it up, the affair was balanced by my taking her Bible. I fear Blackwood & Gordon did not get all my energies next day: whether I worked for my shilling or not must be settled afterwards. I spent a good deal of thought on some lines to put in her Bible, and at night I wrote them on a sheet of paper the very size of her book, and, before slipping them in, I read them to my mother.

She said: " My! Pate, that's guid; I'll let Miss Yule see that."

I felt a bit ashamed. This Miss Yule had only been seen by me as through a glass darkly (she was lodging with a maiden lady on the same landing as ourselves). She knocked at our door one morning, and I answered; there was the mysterious personage closely veiled. When she said in her usual subdued tones: " If you please, this is So-and-So's key," I got an electric shock at the time, which I understood afterwards—*I had met my wife!*"

Miss Yule read the lines, and came to see the author. It was a trying time, and she said: " Did you write that?"

Then I saw her for the first time. I did not think they wondered so much at the verses, as that anything serious should come from such a rattleskull o' a daft laddie. I can re-write them from memory still, and here they are—

>I now return your sacred prize,
>The only foretaste of the skies
>To cheer the soul that panting lies
>   In sin-debased mortality.

It stamps the youth, the father sage,
It cheers the dull, declining age,
It clasps within its sacred page
      The tones of high sublimity.

Oh may its healing virtues flow
Through every vale of life below,
And point the heart oppressed with woe
      To glorious immortality!

Oh may it prove thy constant guide,
Thy faith, thy hope, thy love and pride,
Till launched upon the ebbing tide
      Which bears thee to Eternity!

Then far beyond thy brightest dream,
Far from this sublunary scene,
Thy soul may scan on angel wing
      The bright ethereal canopy.

Yet further still speed on, speed on,
Till 'mid the bright seraphic throng
You join the everlasting song,
      Jehovah's magnanimity.

I had a ruction at Blackwood & Gordon's that I sincerely regret. My engagement with them was for three years by regular indenture, but all matters were not down in black and white. I was to be two years in the finishing department, and the last year at the fitting. The latter was a most important item; we were all anxious to go to sea in the capacity of engineers, not only for the novelty of seeing the world, but also to make some money. When my two years were finished, I made application for the fitting and was refused, the reason assigned being that they had no work for me in that department. This was a sore disappointment, but I made up my mind to accept the inevitable. However, a nephew of Mr. Gordon's, a younger 'prentice than myself, was duly passed into the fitting department, and of course I came to the conclusion that I was being unjustly treated. I lay in wait for the master. "If you please, Mr. Gordon, I would like a word with you."

"Well, what do you want?"

"You will perhaps remember you promised to give me two years at the finishing and one year at the fitting."

"Well?"

"Well, sir, I have only ten months to run of my 'prenticeship, and I have not got to the fitting yet."

"No, and I believe there is no room in that department."

"So they say, but room has been found for a younger man than me, and I don't think it is fair."

I cannot recall all that passed, but I do remember him saying that I seemed to know how to work his business better than he did himself, and that if I was not satisfied, I could leave.

I said, "I'll do that, if you give me my lines."

He said I should get no lines, and left me. While blood is thicker than water, I think the foreman had more to do with it than he had. It was coming near another "social" in connection with our debating and essay class, and my chums were at me for something original as in former years. I thought over it a little, and decided on a piece to be called "A Supper and Presentation to General Gordon, or an hour with the Abercorn Worthies." This gave me an opportunity of mustering all the black boys at a social board, and touching many topics understood only by ourselves. It was mostly harmless banter, except in one or two instances. Mr. Archie Blue (a little deformed man who kept the time), was put in the chair, and all the dignitaries were ranged to right and left. The hardest cut of all was given to the foreman blacksmith. He was a man of prodigious size, and as ungainly in figure as in habits.

> Beside the chairman Vulcan sat,
>   Thrang winkin' on the lassies :
> A man well kent for time misspent
>   In rumplin' fancy dresses.

The chairman rose and said, "Mr. Black would now implore a blessing." This was no less a personage than the senior member of the firm, who was said to be a little sceptical.

> Up Tammie rase and spent a gaze
>   Upon the jovial meeting,
> Syne shook his head and smiling said,
>   "I'm no accustomed speaking
>   'Mang folks at nicht;
>
> "But whan I glower adown the room
>   I think we've blessings plenty,
> To ask for mair is greed, I'm sure—
>   Why, look at ilka dainty!"

Then followed a metrical description of the viands on the table, the finish up of which was,

> "The clan roared oot, Amen."

Toast, song, and sentiment followed, till the chairman called for Pate the Prentice to make the presentation. Pate made his speech, and handed the General a handsomely bound copy of "The Merchant's Guide to Honour." This was followed by the reply, etc., etc.

"Beside the chairman Vulcan sat,
 Thrang winkin' on the lassies."

When the evening came for our social I was simply horrified to see our manager there (he is now a high official with the Board of Trade), and also my own foreman, whom I had characterised as "Wee Johnny." There had never been any but ourselves present on former occasions. Here was I with a piece which took me 25 minutes to deliver, and the rhyme was impossible to alter, and the boys were gasping for it. When my time came, I put everything to the hazard of the die and went straight ahead. I have had many a hearty reception in later life from larger meetings, but never any so boisterous as this one. The jokes and banter were all about kent folk, and appreciated by a lot of fellows glad of any excuse to make a noise. Before the chairman could proceed with the next item, the manager rose and said: "Much as he appreciated the ability of the piece just delivered, he would be wanting in his duty if he did not say he was sorry it had been given, as it threw reflections on an honourable gentleman of which he could not approve."

From that moment a wet blanket fell on the meeting from which it did not recover. The manager came to me to borrow the manuscript, but I asked a night to think it over, and by that time it was baptised with fire. No doubt I did a very foolish thing, and the only excuse I can conjure up is, I was born destitute of common-sense, and during the first twenty years of my life had acquired very little. All sorts of rumours were current in the works as to what was going to be done to me, and I confess I was very much upset, but no one in authority ever said a word to me. I finished my time with the firm and left, but to sea as an engineer I have never been.

Trade was very dull at this time. I was kept on for one month after my apprenticeship was finished, and then " wee Johnnie " came and told me I would have to go. " We've given ye a pey or two to set ye up," he said; " but ye see yersel' there's nae wark: but ye're no needin' to be sae feared as some o' them."

CHAPTER V

Looking for work—The world's end—Charlie Dick—I don't get on with the manager—That besom, Eve—Dundas's tomb—Various misfortunes and trials

> " What anvils rang, what hammers beat!
> In what a forge and what a heat
> Were shaped the anchors of thy hope!"
> —*Longfellow.*

Like most young men in this neighbourhood, I went to Glasgow to look for work. Looking for work is a fine art not to be acquired in a day. Foremen can only be seen at meal-hours, or at six in the evening; perhaps there will be a dozen waiting on the same errand as yourself. You are a stranger, and do not know the man you want when you see him. An old tramp, who knows all the ropes, will generally button-hole the foreman at once, and talk to him all the way till he reaches home, and, if you wait, you may get a word with him on the return journey. You may do two shops at the breakfast hour and two at the dinner, if you are very fortunate, but that is the maximum, and where are you to go from ten o'clock till two? Perhaps into one of the sheds at the Broomielaw, and rest a little. It is wearisome work, and God pity those who have to do it poorly-clad and under-fed. I had three days of it on my first start, and without success. I said to my mother, "That's enough for one week; I'll not go back till Monday." Amid all the distressing circumstances, you sometimes get a laugh too; you meet some real originals on the road. I heard some engineering works discussed, one in Glasgow called the "Slaughter House," well prepared for emergencies, and keeping in the gate-house a web of sticking-plaster and a strauchtin'-board. I was told of another place where, if you could put up with the swearings you got, in three weeks you would likely be the oldest hand in the shop.

Monday came, and I started afresh. I called first on Mr. Archibald Downie, foreman with J. & G. Thomson, Finnieston Street. Downie said he was not in want of any one, but that a friend of his, a Mr. Duncan, in Barclay & Curles', Whiteinch, had told him to send on any likely man. So he said:

"If you like, you can go there, and tell him I sent you."

I thanked him and went at once. I gave Mr. Duncan Mr. Downie's compliments, and got the job, Mr. Duncan saying that it would last only a few weeks.

I started the next day, and got my first experience of lodgings. Ochone! what a change! and I was blate, blate. There was one god-send in my life at this time; Miss Yule, now become Maggie, was staying with her mother in Glasgow, and thither, as to a haven of refuge, I turned in the evenings. The anxiety I had about my work was intense; I was always in dread I would get something to do I was not able for. Yet I succeeded wonderfully, and when the work was finished, Mr. Duncan said:

"Well, Peter, just gang back to Mr. Downie, gie him my compliments, and say I sent ye."

I said, "I doubt it's no use; the man you paid off two days ago was there, and they are not needing anybody."

"Never you mind," he says, "dae what I bid ye."

Accordingly I went to Downie; he had forgotten sending me to Duncan, but listened to my story with apparent interest. He said, "I could gie ye a job, but the stuff's no forrit yet."

"Never mind," I replied, "I'll go home for a fortnight and wait, for I would like to get into your place for the quality of the work."

When I returned, he said, "I am ashamed that things are not much different; however, if you come to-morrow, I'll find something for you."

This was good news, for the place was, and is still, famous for the high-class quality of the work. It is most important for young men when they make a change, to learn, as soon as possible, the class of work wanted, some shops being for quality, and others for speed. I have

The boys often went to the Broomielaw to see the steamer come home.

always had a great admiration for Mr. Downie: he had a fine manner in speaking to the men, never failing to give each one his name, which struck me as equally singular and pleasant. My wages were twenty-one shillings a week; yet I seldom thought of money: the work entranced me. In this place they made a great number of oscillating engines, and Thomson was the maker of all the famous *Ionas* of the Clyde. The boys in the work considered, as much as their masters did, that their honour was bound up in these boats, and often went to the Broomielaw to see the steamer come home.

One of the Thomsons, I think Mr. George, became an officer in the Volunteers, a movement that was very popular at this time. He sent one of the foremen to beat up for recruits, and lectured us on Spartan bravery. I did not feel settled enough to join any corps.

A great revival of religion had also taken place in Scotland. The Wynd Church was crowded every night. Dr. Andrew Bonar gave our men many an address in the works during the dinner-hour, and I have listened to the grand old man many a time.

I saw some great boilers being prepared one day for going to the big crane in order to be put into a boat called the *Adela*. I knew a lot of men would be called out to drag them down a few minutes before six o'clock. I was watching in hopes of being one of them. I was disappointed, and saw with regret the others go off. When we got out at six o'clock, a terrible scene presented itself. The men, when they had got the boilers outside the gate, started at a canter; there would be perhaps one hundred and fifty or so at the ropes. One man fell, and I do not know how many fell over him. Before they could rise, the immense boggie, with wheels fifteen inches broad, came down upon them, and two men were killed, the legs of one of them being spread out like a sheet of paper. How often in this life are our disappointments, blessings in disguise!

One day the foreman brought in a new chum and put him next vice to me. He was a young fellow of about my own age, and many a keek I took at him, wondering who he was and where he came from. In a short time he came boldly over to me and said, "My name is Charles Dick, have you any objection to tell me yours?"

"None in the world," I said, and when he got it, he marched back to his work. I looked after him and said to myself, "My man, you're a queer brick." We became fast friends, and shortly after, he asked me if I was comfortable in my lodgings.

I said, "Just middling."

"Well," he said, "What do you think of us looking for a room and chumming it together?".

I said that I would be very glad. When I left, it nearly broke the heart of the old maid I had been lodging with; she followed me to my new abode and pled with me to come back.

"Oh," she said, "I never thought *you* would leave me."

"I never thought *you* would leave me."

Poor soul! she was old and grey-headed, and struggling with a lot of rowdy and inconsiderate lodgers for a bare existence. I could not go back to her house, not on her account but for the others. I was indeed sorry for her; there are hundreds like her to whom the world is a wilderness of woe, the fear of destitution dogging their steps till a merciful Providence calls them home.

Charlie was a religious chap, and my own inclinations were in that direction. He joined Dr. Eadie's church in Cambridge Street, and I used to go with him to the Doctor's Bible Class; but on Sundays I was always at Paisley.

After I had learned some of Charlie's history, I

said to him one night, "Man, Charlie, I wonder ye werena feared to come and work in a place like Thomson's; it gave *me* great concern, and I had had experience of marine work; but you were fresh from a sma' machine shop in Monifeith."

"Well," said Charlie, "I couldna say I was feared: here's how I looked at it. 'Charlie,' I said to mysel', 'ye ken how to work malleable and cast iron, brass and steel; you may have to put them into different shapes than heretofore, but if the foreman will say what he wants, or gie ye a drawing, I think ye should manage.'"

"Philosopher, again!" I cried, for as soon as I learned he came from Broughty Ferry, I asked him if he knew Dick, the Christian Philosopher, for the book bearing that name was, in my father's estimation, next to the Bible.

Charlie said there were two remarkable Dicks in Broughty Ferry, but that he was a son of Dick the tailor; and that his father's parting gift to every son that left the house, was a razor. As lang as they were a credit to him, they were to shave and keep themselves respectable; and if they didna behave, the razor might be useful in other ways.

The lodgings Charlie and I occupied were at the "World's End," a little street off Finnieston Street, which, I fear, has been absorbed by the new Stobcross docks. The woman we lodged with, was the perfection of cleanliness. The sparkle of her kitchen fire on a winter's evening was one of the most inviting things to be seen in Scotland. She was very pleasant but reserved. Her smile was a momentary twinkle on a background of sorrow. She sighed heavily at times, as Charlie and myself could hear, and we often said she had a history. We never learned much of it from herself, but we came to know that her husband had been a rigger, and was blown from the mast at sea and drowned. A brother of her own had lived with her, a patternmaker to trade, and a born bachelor. He was a quiet, inoffensive man, his one weakness or vice was that he aye got half-fou' on Saturday. Even in drink, he was easy to get on with. One Saturday, after having had his usual, he adjourned to an eating-house to have a tripe supper, and, as Paddy says, "that was the rear of him." He was carried home dead to his sister, and she was a lonely woman indeed. Charlie and I had some fine times of it here, whiles reading each his own book, sometimes reading together. Shakespeare and Longfellow had a lot of attention from us. Charlie had an old Scotch dictionary which gave us great fun at times. We

I DON'T GET ON WITH MANAGER

were both fond of old Scotch songs and ballads. I never saw anybody so fascinated as Charlie was with the "Muckin' o' Geordie's byre." "Ilk dad o' the scartle strak fire," simply set him off in a roar.

My days in Finnieston and my evenings at the "World's End" were pleasant indeed. There was only one thing that marred my pleasure at the work: the manager did not like me. He was a perfect Anak of a man, and far from being bonnie. He would plunge his big fist into his trouser pocket and bring out a museum of things, such as a bunch of keys, a lot of money, his watch and other things, pick out a piece of chalk and draw anything he wanted to describe.

He would plunge his big fist into his trouser pocket.

The other things were transferred to the orifice of the pocket, and you could hear them jaup at the bottom. He was very regular in his habits, and you could reckon to a few minutes when he would appear on his rounds. Yes, and we had eye-servants on our flat, who would watch for him, and when he came, would draw such blows with their hammers, he could hardly get past. I considered this mean, and would not stoop to it, and perhaps I gave him the impression of listlessness. One day I was working at a donkey-engine when he came in. I could not proceed with my work at the moment, as I had discovered some discrepancy between the drawings and the parts I had to manipulate; to use a shop phrase, "they would not come in." I was busy considering what should be done. He stopped beside me: I saw his great legs and feet. I never moved, neither did he: the situation became painful. I looked up and said: "There is something wrong here."

"Why did you not see that before?" he replied, and his great jaws came together like a rat-trap.

I have thought over that question for nearly forty years, and give it up: I can't answer yet. Some time after that, my good foreman Downie came to me quite excited:

"This will never do, Peter, wasting time working with a straight-edge and red lead, at a job like that.

Man, it's only a templet for a paddle-arm to guide the smith in the forging of it."

I had to think a moment to take in the situation, and saw it. I never spoke a word. I lifted the wooden straight-edge and showed him both edges. It told its own story.

" Is that what you are working with ? "

" Yes."

"Dod, the manager flew on me the noo like a lion about you and your red lead," and away he went in disgust.

After being ten months in the place, I thought I was worthy of more wages, but knew it was no use asking, for the manager, and he alone, had power to grant a rise. I resolved to leave, and told some of the men so. One man, who was an old servant, said:

" Well, if you are going to leave, you might do a favour to those who are left: seek up your wages; of course you won't get it, but they are the better of the men complaining now and again. When the manager came here he brought them doon sair enough."

" Oh," I said, " I'll soon seek up my wages."

" If you please," said I to the manager, " I would thank you for an increase of wages."

" How much have you ? "

" Twenty-one shillings."

" Well, you have plenty : if not content, *gv*."

" Thanks." I *goed*.

Notice to leave can only be received at the pay-table. I never saw that table. There is something humiliating in the manner working-men are paid. You are called by number like convicts, and a tin box is pushed through a hole at you like a dog's breakfast. I had to stoop down and call through the aperture, " Please accept my notice to leave."

An elderly man, who was paid after me, and to whom I had never spoken, touched me on the shoulder.

" You've gien in your warning ? "

" Yes."

" Hae ye got anither job ? "

" No."

" Oh, callan, ye shouldna dae that. I've had six months o't and ken what it is."

Poor soul ! he was very subdued ; but I had no burden to carry at that time except myself, and out of my twenty-one shillings a week, I had been laying away a goodly sum.

While I was working my warning, which seemed the longest two weeks I had ever wrought, one of the men said to me, " Away alang to Lancefield ; Napier is wanting men."

I went one meal-hour and was offered work, but they would not wait a week for me. I spoke to Downie about it.

" Well, Peter," he said, " if you were going to sea, or *said* you were leaving the country, I could let you away, but not otherwise."

" Well," I said, " I'm doing neither, and will just work it out and trust to Providence."

A few minutes before we stopped on the last Saturday I was with them, he came to me and said, " Weel, Peter, ye're makin' things snod."

I was brushing down the bench and said, " Yes ; and I am sorry too."

" If ever you are in want o' wark again, and I can help ye, I'll be very glad."

Good old Downie ! it was not very long till he left himself, and went to Jack's at Liverpool. Archie was a good friend to me, and I have no doubt his example has taught me to be considerate to others.

The last day I was with Thomson, one of my mates said :

" Go to Napier's in Washington Street on Monday, and don't ask them in a general way for a job ; but tell them ye made the donkeys in Thomson's. Napier's donkey-man has been made foreman, and his place has not been filled up yet."

I went and got the job, and was once more a stranger in a strange land. In all my wanderings, I never saw an engineer working with spectacles on but here. Where the old men go, I have never found out, but this old chap was a rarity in more ways than one. Some have great sympathy for a new-comer, and it is all needed. My old friend had a pleasant word and a joke for me. He took a step to me one day, and drawing his fingers across his brow till the sweat ran in beads to the points, he said :

"Is that no awfu'."

"Is that no awfu'; had it no been for that besom, Eve, 1 micht have been lyin' my length the day, birslin' on the Braes o' Paradise."

We were set to work in this place from six A.M. till nine P.M., with the usual meal-hours, of course, and half-an-hour for tea at six P.M. I could not go to my lodgings and back in that time, and being offered work in Paisley, I left, serving Napier only two weeks.

I was several months in Paisley in a shop where part of the old Infirmary now stands, and, strange to say, employed by the man who had been my first foreman, he being now in business for himself. His younger brother, who was in partnership with him, and with whom I was very pack, said to me:

"Gie in your warning the morn, Pate, and tak' the wind oot o' Bob's sails; for there's naething he likes so much as paying off men, and he has you on the list."

I did as I was bid, and the young fellow got a jolly row, and was accused of conveying information. There was nothing for it but to go in search again. I was anxious to remain in Paisley for the sake of the old folks, and got into a machine-shop in the town. This was the shop of Mr. Dundas, a famous machinist. Dundas was a character, and so were many of his workmen. He had a grand blacksmith called Sawney Ross, the quietest man I was ever near when he was sober, and the noisiest when drunk, which was oftener than should have been. I heard him go through the place one day in an intoxicated condition, singing his loudest:

> "Life is the season God has given,
> To rise from Hell and fly to Heaven."

He was full of Scripture, and one day caught Dundas in his arms, and said:

"Black but comely like the daughters of Jerusalem."

Dundas built a grand tomb for himself in Paisley Cemetery. The covering of the vault being made of a series of heavy iron plates fitted so close as to be air-tight. It is said that he went to the vault one day, raised one of the plates and descended. The cover had not been properly secured, and it fell back into place, and there had near been a tragedy. When anxiety had been roused about his absence, the vault was visited, and the man found at his last gasp. He was sufficiently recovered next day to go for the man for not making a better job of it, or he (Dundas) could not have lived so long. Let us hope this is exaggerated. There was no fun, however, in this place for me; it was the most unfortunate place I ever had. For one thing, the work was entirely strange to me, and my confidence was shaken. I had no pleasure on account of my anxiety. The foreman was a peculiar man, of few words as a rule. He gave me a stinging vote of censure the second day. Every shop has its own mode of working, and in this shop a man did not require to mark his time as in some places; the time-keeper came round and took it from each worker *vivâ voce*.

"Well," he said to me, "what were you at yesterday?"

I did not know the number of job; I looked round and saw the foreman in a distant part of the flat. I went to him and asked him what I should mark. He never spoke but walked across the shop with dignified leisure, turned over one of the articles, pointed to No. 23 marked on it with chalk, and left it in supreme silence. A very severe reproof was administered to me by his manner. Cruel Scotland! two days after that, I broke a three-eighths tap; such a thing has been done before even by a journeyman, and will happen again. But, oh! how gladly I would have paid for it, for I fell further in his estimation than the value of a dozen taps. Time passed, but I never reached calm and composure. A man called Hugh Robertson, considered a crack hand, saw my excitement and said to me, "You are getting on well enough with that job for the time you are at it."

Hugh should have been a good judge, for he was taken not long after this to be foreman with the Boyds of Shettleston. But I could never see a gleam of satisfaction in the gaffer, and felt miserable.

A man had been discharged who had been working on some mill-gearing, and I was set to it next. Though I had never done work of the kind before, I had a good idea of how to proceed: it was to hang and key a big bevel wheel. It was first staked up with wedges till it would turn perfectly true; four keys were then fitted and the wedges withdrawn. I had got it staked fair, and went to the pattern-maker's shop to make the keys in wood for the guidance of the smith, who was to make them in iron. Engineers have no wood-working tools of their own, and I had to borrow. Pattern-makers do not like to lend their tools more than they can help. I made the wood templets as near as possible to measurement, took them away to the job, and was giving them the final touch with the file. The foreman attacked me like a terrier for that; he went and brought an old plane, the iron of which was worn down to the nail-slot and broken through. It was useless; I finished with the file, and he made the smith work late to forge the keys.

I was telling the old folks at home how dismal the outlook was, and mother counselled patience.

"Oh, ha'e patience, Pate."

"I ha'e taken the last," I said, "and the next will finish it."

I was in next morning sharp at six, got my keys and went to the grind-stone to break the skin, as we term it (a fresh forging spoils a file). When the foreman came in, he made straight for me.

"What are you doing here?"

I did not like the question, as he could see for himself. "I am grinding the keys."

"You are doing anything and everything to waste your time," said he, and walked away and left me.

I drew a long breath, and went after him.

"It's very evident, sir, I cannot please you, and the sooner I leave you the better."

"Who could be pleased?" he said, and then he gave me all my faults he had been treasuring up, the filing of wood among the rest. We were walking through the shop all the time, and the men were taking stock of the play. We had reached my bench, and I took up the plane he had given me, turned it upside down as joiners do when they want to withdraw the iron, and struck it a smash on the bench that made him start. The iron and wedge were in my hand; I held up the former to him and said, "How could I work with that?"

"Don't spoil the tools," he said.

"I've struck my last blow for you, sir, and I'll sit here till I get my wages."

I got them, and was home before breakfast-time. It seems I should have taken the keys to the grinder, a man who worked only at the stone. I never was in a shop before or since where this was the law; and I would have kept the law if I had known it. This was a sore episode in my life, and I was long in getting over it. I have met the man in later life, and given him share of our work too.

Nature was not in want of a gentleman when I was born, so I had to take the road again. It's wonderful what one hears when moving about.

A fellow-tradesman said to me, "Try Davie Broon."

This Mr. Brown had charge of the Glasgow and South-Western Locomotives at Bridge Street Station, Glasgow. He spoke very nicely to me and said he was not in want: "But I'm expecting Mr. Montgomery from Kilmarnock, and ye micht get a job from him."

I went back and saw Mr. Montgomery, and he engaged me to start next day. So to Killie I went.

I had to take the road again.

CHAPTER VI

Kilmarnock—Jack Smith—My landlord—Dan Fraser—Hammerman's strike—An engine off the line—Father and son—Jamie Cree—The Christian Israelites—Two misers—Jamie M'Kie—I get settled and become restless—Prayer meetings in a tenement

> " Go, Fame, and canter like a filly,
>   Through a' the streets and neuks o' Killie!"
> —*Burns.*

What a change, my countrymen! I thought I had landed in the Garden of Eden when I landed in Kilmarnock, such nice, civil people to serve, and I passed waving corn-fields on the way to the work, and what a magnificent work! The men were divided into squads. Every squad had two locomotives. The squad was composed of four or five engineers, a leading man and a labourer.

I was set to work with a little man called Jack Smith, who belonged originally to Perth. I felt at home with him from the first. Jack's only fault was that he took an occasional spree, which might last from three days to a week, yet the Company put up with him. Unfortunately, his wife was more addicted to drink than himself. Jack and I got on fine, but never in our lives had we a dram together. He was a loveable man in many ways. I lent him a little money once which he never paid, but I never grudged it. He was in an awful state when he came to borrow it; he said: "I do not know what to do; my daughter is to be married to-night, and the mother simply not presentable."

I always felt that but for her Jack would do well, and with the rashness of youth said, "Jack, you should leave her."

He looked at me very solemn for a moment and said, "I couldna dae that: *it was me that learned her.*"

I was fortunate in securing good lodgings in Kilmarnock, and made no change till I went to a house of my own. My landlord—Alexander Hamilton—was country-bred, and, in all matters relating to farm-life and kitchen-gardening, an expert. He had come to town, like other peasants, because better wages were to be had, and the prospect of a better outlook for his family. I don't think I ever saw him reading anything except his Bible and the local papers.

"Mony a book," he said to me, "you read, but I ken ane ye never read."

"What is that?" I enquired.

He struck an attitude, and said, "'This bonnie mornin', Roger, cheers my bluid——'"

"Yes," I answered, "'An' puts a' nature in a jovial mood.'"

"Tae the de'il wi' ye—ye ken everything."

Sandy had once taken part in playing Allan Ramsay's *Gentle Shepherd*, and I don't think he ever committed anything else to memory.

To trade he was a sawyer—not a top sawyer, but a bottom one. Of all the trades which machinery has displaced, this one should be the least grudged. Five minutes of it put the strongest in a flood of perspiration. Sandy was a strong, thick-set, hardy little man, with a fell of hair that might have rivalled Esau's; and how cheerily did he toil to fill the mouths and cleed the backs o' weans and wife.

One night, at his kitchen fireside, he said to me, "Read us a bit, man; read us a bit. We are feared tae speak for disturbin' ye, and there ye sit drinkin' in everything yoursel'."

I was feeling how little I had got at school, and

was trying at this time to plough my way through Euclid. I read him the first proposition, and asked him if I would proceed.

"Goodness, no," he replied. "I never heard sic a rigmarole o' blethers a' my born days."

His wife was a jewel of a woman—tall and gentle, her complexion eloquent of the farm and fresh air. I was wicked enough to try several times to ruffle her temper, and only once partly succeeded, when I belittled her minister.

I remember coming in one Saturday evening about eight o'clock, after a long walk. The kitchen looked so inviting that I brought my book, and sat down by the fire. The sparkle of the flame was beautiful on the polished fire-irons. Her week's work was finished—the floor, made of fire-clay tiles, was washed and sanded; the children's Sunday clothes were hanging on the chair-backs ready for the coming day, and all the boots brushed; the children a-bed, but not sleeping, and she herself deep in the *Kilmarnock Post*. I soon found I could not read for the racket going on in one of the beds. I glanced at the mother: she was the figure of perfect peace. I looked to the bed: it was a kaleidoscope. Pillows were flying, and legs and arms mixing and separating like a country dance, and the noise was appalling.

It was far more interesting than any book, and I set myself to see how long that gentle mother would stand it. But at last there came a cry there was no mistaking—some one was hurt. She turned her head from her paper and said, " What's wrang wi' ye, Lizzie?"

And after a sob or two, Lizzie said, " Maggie scartit me."

" Never mind, hinney," said the mother, " it will save ye daein't yersel'!"

A fellow-workman asked me if I was a member of the Amalgamated Engineers' Society.

" Yes," I replied.

" Well, you ought to report yourself to the Secretary, Dan Fraser."

Dan was in the same department as myself. I was greatly struck with this man, his appearance, voice, and gentlemanly manners. Dan was a good scholar, and should have been a journalist. As it was, he did a lot of reviewing for old M'Kie of the *Kilmarnock Post*.

A young man in the turning-shop was putting on the belt of his lathe, and had his arm torn away from the shoulder. He had been ten months in the society, but members are not entitled to benefit during the first year. Had the accident taken place two months later, he would have received from the society £100. Dan at once took the matter up, and made a touching appeal to all the branches, and the response was about £120. That, with the assistance from the railway people, gave the lad close upon £140. He opened a public-house, which in two years wrecked the moral man worse than the shaft did the physical.

Many years after I had left Killie, I met an old acquaintance and inquired after Dan.

"Dan," he says, "is in Constantinople, and the way he got there is like a romance. Being secretary of the society he had many callers. One day at the dinner hour a man came inquiring for work. Dan thought he looked weary and broken-down like, so took him in and gave him his dinner, but no prospect of work in Kilmarnock. Long after, an advertisement appeared in the local papers for an engineer to go to Turkey. Dan applied and got the job. He was met before he left the steamer at Constantinople by the man he had dined, and who was now to be his master. The latter had forgotten Dan's name, fished for him by advertisement and caught him. Some time after, Dan came back to the Railway Company, and died in the town of Irvine.

Patrick Stirling, superintendent, Pat, as he was familiarly called, was a man much respected by all. He was bluff and straight: tradesmen don't like diplomats. His voice was seldom heard, and I would never have heard it but for the fact that I called upon him in his private room. The Company had been in the habit of giving free passes to their workmen, but it was beginning to be overdone, which I did not know. I was assured I had no more ado than ask for one, so I ventured.

"What are you going to Glasgow for?"

"I am going to see a relative who is very ill."

"I don't know what things are coming to," he said. "One has a faither deein', another has a sister that will never get better, and a third's gaun tae bring hame a widowed dochter. The fac' is, Glasgow's gaun a' tae the devil thegither."

Patrick Stirling.

I was glad to get out, and can't remember whether I got the pass or not; very likely I did.

Pat was a man considerably over six feet. He walked through the shop with his chin resting on his breast, looking neither to right nor left; but we scarcely ever failed to know when he was in by the noise Geordie Lorimer made, who had charge of the tenders. Geordie was aye needing the travelling crane when Pat came in. "Come awa' wi' that cran," he would cry. "D'ye think it's a sodger's burial ye're at?" "There noo, that'll dae;" "Lower awa';" "Haud on;" "Cannie you at the front;" "That's hit noo; heave, baith thegither; fine, man!" I often wondered if managers were caught with chaff like that.

One day the hammermen in the smiths' shop came out on strike. I do not remember the matter in dispute. When Mr. Stirling came to the works after ten A.M., they were all congregated at the gate. Some conversation ensued, and Patrick was delivering himself forcibly. He caught sight of one of the men, an Irishman, to whom he had been very kind in various ways. "Are you amang them tae, ye scoundrel?" he roared, and took a running kick at him.

Paddy was smart, but not so smart as the superintendent. There was a howl, and the Irishman ran to safe quarters. Holding one hand consolingly on the injured part, he cried, " Oh, Mr. Stirling, Mr. Stirling, you are the funny man! Yourself made me a present of them trousers, and now you have kicked the seat out of them." It was such a sudden descent to the ridiculous that every one lost his gravity, and the strike was settled in a few minutes, and the works restored to their normal condition.

Word came to the works one day that Engine No. so-and-so was off the line near Dalmellington. The engine was only a few days out of the shop, and was one of the handsomest in the service. The news passed from mouth to mouth like wild-fire, and before we could recover from the shock, Montgomery came down one side of the shop beckoning one after another. All eyes were fixed on him. I got the signal, and my joy was full. We all went to the outside, and John addressed us in these words: " Awa' hame an' get a bite o' dinner, chaps, an' be back here in hauf-an-hour, an' we'll hae a special train tae tak' ye tae the place."

I was back in plenty of time, for I lived near. There was the train, consisting of two third-class carriages (saloon), only out on Glasgow Fair Saturdays, and two trucks loaded with wooden blocks.

"Yourself made me a present of them trousers!"—Page 102.

There was a gang of surfacemen, and perhaps a dozen of engineers. The navvies had their own special tools, and so had we: hammers, chisels, ropes, screw-jacks, crow-bars, etc. We all got in, and away we went down the Troon line, but where we shunted on to the other line, I can't say. We were all as merry as if it had been the Grozet Fair. The carriage was open from end to end, the backs of the seats being only four or five feet high. We could see and converse with each other. I had a good look round; we were a greasy lot; our own wives and sweethearts would have blushed to meet us; but we were the very men for the job, and of more service to the unfortunate engine than if the Company had turned out the Presbytery of Ayr. The oil-can was very busy on the way, and the screw-jacks put into grand fettle. Our train began to slow, and finally stopped. We got out as fast as possible. The sight was pathetic. There lay the giant, his left shoulder burrowed into the embankment, the fires out, and life extinct. What possibilities of power, and what abject helplessness! There was a moral in the picture, and I felt it. We got speedily to business. It was long before we could get the screws in, and, when we did, the blocks of wood began to sink, the ground being soft; but as one block sank, we put another on the top, old Jamie remarking, "'There's ground at the bottom,' says Brian O'Linn."

The foreman, just to rally the men, said, "Jamie, I doot she's gaun tae beat ye."

"Will she?" says Jamie. "Ye ken fine, Mr. Johnstone, if I had the screws richt, I'll either bring that engine up, or *I'll shove the world doon.*"

That was all that was wanted; the men's spirits got a lift. The screws wrought with a lever and ratchet motion, and a rope could be attached to the lever, at which half-a-dozen of us could get a pull. And how we responded when the gaffer cried, "All together, lads!" But when the sun went down, and the chaffers were lit, it was not so cheery. We got the engine up in the small hours of the morning, and the surfacemen laid a branch line below it; when that was finished, we lowered the screws, and she was on the metals again. The pilot-engine soon dragged her on to the main line. We got home about six in the morning, and brought the prodigal with us.

There was a re-arrangement of hands, and I was shifted from Jack Smith to Jamie Jeffrey. I did not like the change; the two men were as different as June and December. Jamie was the most fastidious man I ever knew; but he could only bark, or nobody would have stayed with him. He could lose his temper two or three times in a forenoon, and as often get it back again. When he scolded a man, he was straightway struck with remorse, and his attempts to make up the peace were as aggravating as his insolence. One day he gave me a jolly row for daring to sharpen a drill. Soon he came slipping to my neighbourhood, as if he were looking for something, and whispered, " I believe she said that."

I knew his tactics; he wanted me to ask " What did she say?" But I was still at red heat, so I replied, " I don't give a —— what she said, and don't come to me with your stories till you learn how to treat men."

But you could not be angry with Jamie long; he would not let you. He was a good tradesman, painstaking and perfect in his work, and his engines much appreciated.

The general tool-chest, which, with every other squad, was open to all the members, was kept by Jamie under lock and key, and he never grudged to come out of the pit, or down from the top of the engine, to give you what was wanted; but I never saw a hand in the box except his own. He could go into it in the dark and get anything he wanted.

One day, his son and only child, a fellow of eighteen or nineteen, was working below the engine. He was trying to take off a thin nut; the key he had was not suitable, and he asked his father for another. The father replied that it was not another key but a man that was wanted. "Say you can't do it, and I'll do it myself."

"I can't do it," cried the loon.

The father was up to forty pounds in a minute; he caught hold of the side-rod of the engine, swung his legs into the pit, and cried, "Gie me the key."

The key did the same with the father as it did with the son. It slipped, but the father, being in a rage, was less cautious, and struck himself on the face and bled his nose. We all laughed, son included. Jamie could not stand that from the lad, and struck him a stinging blow on the body. It was a warm corner; the father bleeding, and the son gasping for breath. By and by, the young man made his way out. The father looked through the spokes of the driving wheel and said, "I'll learn ye to lauch at me."

"Aye," said the son, "many a lesson ye've gi'en me, father; but d'ye ken this, ye're just a ——— auld wife."

The father was out the pit in an instant, but the

son dared him, saying, "I've taken my last blow from ye, and if ye strike me, I'll strike ye back."

There was one 'prentice in the squad, whose name was Jamie Cree. He and I were good friends. He was as thoughtless as most young fellows, and sometimes I took him to task. The Revival was in full swing in Kilmarnock at this time, and many notable cases of conversion took place which were of an enduring nature. One afternoon, I saw a noted revivalist cross the shop and speak to Jamie. I said, " What on earth has come up Johnnie Auld's back that he would be seen speaking to a sinner like you."

" Oh," he said, " he was asking me to a meeting."

" And are you going ? "

" Yes," and he laughed.

Next day I asked, " Well, what about the meeting ? "

" It was down at Landsborough's Kirk."

" Wha was speaking ? "

" Tam Falconer, the collier. I think Johnnie had been telling him about me," said Jamie ; but in reality it was conscience at work : " The spirit of a man is the candle of the Lord."

" What was the subject ? " I asked.

" How long halt ye between two opinions ? " he replied.

"Well, have ye made up your mind?"

"I think I have."

Jamie was a changed man; the tables were turned, for now he lectured me. He left his trade when his time was finished, and went to the Holm Mission in Kilmarnock; he taught an infant class, the Rev. Mr. Banks giving him in return the rudiments of Latin and Greek. He is now a minister in New Zealand.

To give even a cursory review of all the people I met and knew, would fill a volume, but I cannot expect them to have the interest for others that they still possess for me. There was a relation of Robert Burns in the railway shop, called John Begg, a very old man, and very proud of his relationship. He once handled a hammer for me, which I kept for some years, but it has gone amissing.

We had two Christian Israelites in the work. These characters never cut their hair; it was put up like a woman's, and stowed away somewhere in their bonnets. The eldest of the two, Jamie Cumming, who worked a circular saw, was an interesting individual. He was the most remarkable man in the Scriptures I ever tackled. When he preached in public, as he did every Sunday, he always had with him a copy of Cruden's *Concordance*, so that if any one raised a question, he could appeal at once to the Law and to the Testimony.

The first time that I saw him, was at a friend's house, where I was visiting. Before I had been

The two Christian Israelites.

many minutes in, he said, " What is your opinion of the common and the great Salvation ? "

I was staggered by the question, but said, " Are they not one and the same ? *Great* on account of the magnitude of the work, and *common* because common to all believers ? "

He took such a sympathising look at me. "Oh, man, but you're far wrang; the *common* salvation is the salvation of the spirit, for," said he, "the spirit returneth to God who gave it." (Here he gave chapter and verse.)

According to Jamie, the Great Salvation is the salvation of body, soul, and spirit; he further maintained that body and soul both went to the grave. This I would not accept, and quoted from Revelations the passage telling how John saw and heard the souls under the altar, saying, "How long, O Lord, holy and true, wilt Thou not avenge our blood upon those that dwell upon the earth?"

"That's it," said Jamie. "Is an altar not a place for sacrifice?"

"Yes."

"Was Christ not the greatest sacrifice ever offered?"

"Yes."

"Was He not offered on the Cross?"

"Yes."

"Was that not on the earth?"

"Yes."

"Well, the souls were under the altar and, therefore, in the grave."

Jamie loved to lead you along a path such as that,

taking your answer as you went; but I got old-fashioned for him by and by. You could not but respect the man: he was sincere and consistent, and fully believed he would live till the Saviour's second coming, and was making himself ready.

His only disciple, Peter, was not so robust, by a long way. I never cared so much for him. One day he said to me, "'Let us go forth to Him without the camp bearing his reproach;' that's the Beard," he said, "and nothing but the Beard."

My reply was, "Does not Nature itself teach you that it is a shame for a man to have long hair?"

"Yes, yes," he said. "Nature teaches that, but Grace never."

There was an essay club in the work, which was broken up shortly before I arrived. Peter gave an essay to this class, the subject being, "The Third Heavens." I cannot give a full account of the proceedings, not having been present; but Peter, it seems, maintained that Adam was the First Heavens, Noah the Second, and our Saviour the Third.

When he had finished, there was absolute silence, and no one seemed inclined to criticise it. At length, Bob Campbell rose; he was leading man of the new engines, a man of few words, but strong common-sense. "Mr. Chairman," said Bob, "certain strange things have been brought to our ears to-night, things I can neither follow nor fathom. I will not dwell on the First nor the Third Heavens; but if Noah was the Second, some part of him must have been the windows thereof, and Peter would have done us a service if he had told us whether the Patriarch *grat* the Flood or *spewed* it!"

We had also two men at the railway works who were reported to be misers. One was old and the other young. Auld Willie was a quiet, inoffensive man. I do not think I ever heard the sound of his voice, and would have paid no attention to him, except that I heard the youngsters cry as he passed, "Sour Kail!" He lived, as Paddy would say, "all alone by himself." It was said he made as much broth every Sunday as lasted him for a week, a due proportion of which he carried every working day to the works for dinner.

The young one was of a different stamp. Jamie was very reserved and, although he was taunted sore, displayed that charity which beareth all things. Although he was a shareholder in the Company, it did not prevent the apprentices from shying a dirty piece of waste at his head whenever they had a chance. His wages were 24s. a week, and it was affirmed he lived on the 4s. and saved the pound; and out of the 4s. he paid 2s. for his lodgings. I have no doubt the report was very near the truth. He was at that time building large tenement property in Glasgow, and went on foot on the Saturday afternoons, to see how the work was progressing. I have seen him start off in grand trim, but at the burgh boundary he stripped himself of shoes and stockings, and did the remainder of the tramp barefoot. I need not add that he also walked back again.

Jamie, the miser.

On the coldest winter day that blew (and the shop was draughty), Jamie's shirt-sleeves were rolled up to the arm-pits. He was in good flesh, but his arms looked sometimes like mottled soap. I made up my mind to speak with this man, but he was as shy as a corncraik, and I laid the siege carefully for a month or two. He assisted an old man, whose name I forget, at the hydraulic machine for taking the axles out of waggon and engine wheels. I spoke to this old man at times—ignoring Jamie—and at a suitable moment also addressed him; thus by inches got his confidence. He held the ordinary workman and his extravagance in supreme contempt. "Hoo can they," he said, "stan' up for their rights? They waste every penny they earn, and if it comes to a strike, they are in starvation in a fortnicht, an' a' they are worth in their uncle's."

But for my curiosity to speak with this man, I might have passed unnoticed the machine they were working at. It was a powerful tool and served as an illustration to me of other operations. One day I was standing by when they were taking the axle out of a pair of wheels. Two strong arms laid hold of the wheel while the ram was brought to bear on the axle; the pump was applied till the gauge registered some hundreds of pounds pressure to the square inch. The old man looked at it and said, "If ye'll no gang at that, we'll hae tae coax ye." So he lifted a hand hammer and gave the tire a tap, and a slight vibration being produced, the shaft was out in an instant.

It was to me an apt illustration of the great revival going on in the country. Every other night, the word of an illiterate preacher was turning a sturdy sinner into a sober, decent, religious man. We wondered at the power of the evangelist, forgetting that the Spirit of God had put the pressure on the sinner.

I had great difficulty in finding any one in the work who so much as knew Miss Aird the poetess, and as I had a high opinion of some of her pieces, such as "The Herd Laddie" and "The Auld Kirkyard," I was anxious to see the lady. By and by I got to know her, and saw her often. I also called on Archibald Mackay, author of "My First Bawbee," and bought something from him, but my chief object was to see and speak with him, though I did not reveal my intention. Jamie M'Kie, publisher of the *Kilmarnock Post*, and a great Burns collector, was another noted character. Dan Fraser, before mentioned, told me that when he first came to work in Kilmarnock, he wrote a letter to his wife to apprise her of his safe arrival, and then sauntered out to look at the town and post his letter. He went into M'Kie's shop and said to the magnate himself, "Would you please give me a postage stamp?"

Jamie's answer was, "I'll see you —— first."

Nevertheless, the two grew to be great friends,

and many a volume Dan reviewed for Jamie's paper. I remember Jamie incurring the wrath of a lady secularist who came to lecture in one of the halls.

"I'll see you —— first:"

The lady had her revenge on him at a meeting at which I was present. The head and front of his offending was what he said in noticing her meeting: "I do not like she-infidels."

I GET SETTLED AND BECOME RESTLESS

Altogether I was much pleased with Kilmarnock. Life at the Railway Works was pleasant, though the reward was small. I began to think seriously of making the town my home. A shop-mate, who must have been a thought-reader, laid his hand on my shoulder one day and said, " Man, Pate, if ye want tae enjoy the greatest happiness wi' the least pleasure, get mairrit." And after our laugh was over, another said, " Joking aside, it is the best thing you could do; and mark my words, your money will go further in a home of your own than ever it did in lodgings." That man was a true prophet: I could always keep track of my money in lodgings, but in my own home I could not follow it with a telescope.

It was the lot of Maggie and myself to be far apart, and our courtship was mostly by letter. I believe we knew each other's thoughts and principles all the better. While she was a very cheerful woman, she was also deeply religious. We had exchanged crooked bawbees on the evening of our engagement, 16th March, 1857; both coins are still in evidence. She also gave me a New Testament, which is worn done. She wrote out from time to time lists of passages of Scripture, which we agreed to read at the same hour each evening; and while she was in Stirling, and I in Kilmarnock, it brought us for a short season each day together in spirit. Prior to going to Stirling, she had opened a shop in Main Street, Gorbals, Glasgow. The shop was furnished by our mutual savings. It did not succeed. There was no failure; every one was paid out, and the place closed. We began to save again, and out of 22s. per week, I laid away almost every fortnight £1. When we had somewhere about £30 saved, we took up house at No. 1 Inkerman Place. It was a room and kitchen. We were married in Glasgow, at her mother's, on the 28th June, 1861. When I brought her home, she sat down at her own fireside, and had a good cry. It was not sorrow but joy. She had been knocked about from pillar to post for many years, and now having a home of her own, however humble, was overwhelming.

My wife was brought up at a boarding-school from a child. Her widowed mother was housekeeper to one of our Scotch nobility. She was afterwards sent to the Normal at Edinburgh, and while still a girl, was installed as mistress of a school by the Countess of Buchan. Her education was much superior to anything I could lay claim to, and no doubt helped to draw forth the admiration I felt for her. She was early matured, and joined the Church at twelve years of age, and continued a consistent and devoted servant of Christ till she went home. I am only realising now how long I entertained an angel unawares. What an influence that woman had on my life; I was nothing but a rollicking, harum-skarum run-a-gate, as my mother used to say. Never ask me that question, " Is marriage a failure?" The days I spent in the two-roomed houses, and in houses of only one, were the happiest of all my life, and if Heaven is to be a patch on them, may we all get there!

Our first boy was born at Inkerman Place, on the 3rd May, 1862. Before his advent, my wife nearly broke my heart by opening a drawer, and showing me all clothing necessary for her last toilette, in the event of her death during the ordeal.

On the 28th May, we removed to Hamilton Street to a smaller house, the rent at Inkerman Place being more than we could afford. This gave me my first fit of restlessness. A dog's life I could get at Killie, " hunger and ease," but, like Oliver, I wanted more. I, therefore, took what may be described as a mental fever, a thing as common to men of from twenty to twenty-five, as measles or whooping-cough to children. I discovered I had gone to the wrong occupation. This disease is frequent among tradesmen. During the first years of apprenticeship, the mind is comparatively easy, but when journeymanship is near, and you know you are about to be launched on the world as a separate and responsible entity, you begin to take stock, and find, like Old Mother Hubbard, that the cupboard is bare. This is especially the case in engineering: you know so little, you have so much to learn, you feel that you are so dull a scholar, there is no doubt about it you are at the wrong business, and you have no natural qualification for the trade. You think you would have succeeded so much better had you gone to something else. I searched all the advertisements I could lay hands on, and was nearly applying for a job as a book-canvasser, which if I had got, the first four hours would have finished it. Still, I continued to search as for hid treasures, looking on all hands for light, with a faith amounting to superstition. Light came; a piece of paper was one day blown to my feet, on which were printed these words, "If you have made a mistake in choosing your business, don't make a second by forsaking it." I looked upon this as a revelation, and from that day to this have never desired a change. Young men! if you cannot succeed at the business you have partly learned, how do you expect to succeed at one you know nothing about?

I heard of a Paisley man who went to work at the Malta gas-works, and had been retained. I came to the conclusion to seek work with a firm of gas engineers in hope of similar luck; but I would not leave one place till I had another, so we stayed a year more in Hamilton Street. At last I got work in Paisley, and when leaving the good-wife, the neighbours said: "Now, don't lose time coming back to flit; we will see a' your things on the train and the wife safe aff!" and they did. Working-men have not much to give, but, like the apostles of old, you are welcome to what they have. I think I should say a word for Hamilton Street before I leave it. The tenement in which I lived, had ten tenants. Some of my friends said, when they heard I was going there, "Man, ye're just gaun tae a barracks." I wish there were more places like it. We were mostly young couples, engineers, painters, boiler-makers, locomotive drivers, railway porters, etc. Every house nearly having little children, we could not go to the church prayer meeting, so we had one of our own in each other's houses week about. I have carried my first-born in his cradle upstairs, and Maggie coming behind me with the Bible. Ach, it was not only grand, it was glorious; no stair-head battles in that land!

CHAPTER VII

A DOWN-AT-THE-HEEL-MECHANIC—LIFE IN DERRY—NED FARREN AND HIS OWLD HORSE—I BECOME A SHAREHOLDER IN "THE SPURTLE"—THE FAMILY LIFE OF MR. ROSS, FOREMAN—HOW HE POPPED THE QUESTION

"'Do you mean to tell us that it will be possible to have a light without a wick?'
"'Yes, indeed, I do.'"
—*W. Murdoch.*

I HAD made two rules for my conduct which took some fortitude to carry out—one was never to lose a moment of working time, and the other never to drink with my fellow-workers or anybody else during the day. So when I started in Paisley, I went at six A.M.; and I do not think the foreman liked it; for I was there at least half-an-hour before he was. I was put to work with a leading man, who was the greatest specimen of a down-at-the-heel mechanic I have ever met. I soon got into his bad graces on account of the last resolution named, but I endeavoured to redeem my position by working hard.

Trade was busy, and we worked till 8 P.M. every night; I was glad of that—it meant more money, and that was needed. About three months before leaving Kilmarnock, I had removed from Hamilton Street to the " Square " (Company's houses). I had done so on purpose, so that when I got work out of town, I should not have a house on my hands. When a worker left the Company's service, he left the house also. I got a home in Paisley; but as I required to purchase some things for it, I wanted to leave my work one evening at six P.M. for that purpose. The leading man referred to objected, and would not let me go. I appealed to the foreman, who said I was foolish to flit to Paisley, as I might not be long with them. This gave me a lump in my throat, and I suspected the drouthy had been undermining me. I explained all the circumstances to John Craig, the foreman, and he let me go. John and I grew very friendly as time wore on, and we held each other in mutual respect. He was a total abstainer, and highly esteemed by all those who knew him or served him.

Some time after this, a sensation was caused in the works by a gentleman calling for our dissipated leading man. The two paced up and down the yard for an hour or more. What a contrast!

One was handsomely dressed, and so gentlemanly like; the other like a tattie-bogle. It leaked out that the gentleman represented a large forging

The two paced up and down the yard.

establishment on the Clyde, and had come to give dilapidated Daunie another chance there, on the condition that he should be a total abstainer. The "wreck," of course, promised, and no doubt determined to make another attempt to arrest his downward career.

I was greatly astonished at night, after having had tea and a good wash, to see Daunie's brother come into my kitchen. He said—" Peter, you will wonder to see me here; but, do ye ken, oor Daunie has got the offer o' his job back at the forge, and he is to bring a man wi' him capable of keeping the steam-hammers in order. It will be a fine place— little to do during the day, but plenty after the men quit. Daunie was wondering if you would go with him." I asked a night to think it over. As my regard for the man was utterly destroyed by his petty persecution of me for the very principles he was now clinging to, I could not go, and gave my decision accordingly. "The king may come the cadger's road yet."

We had some strange characters in the work. Trade was brisk, and some very indifferent men were there, who would not have found employment at other times. We had an old cynic from Glasgow, a poor tradesman, whom the boys nick-named "the flesher." He had a waff o' Tam Carlyle about him. He hated Paisley, and that did not help him with those who had been born there.

"Sic a like place," he would say; "lo'd, there's

naething tae see; in some toons when your wark's dune, you can gang oot an' look at something; but Paisley can shew you naething but Tannahill's hole."

Irishmen were also his aversion, and that did not sweeten his lot where so many were employed.

"Paddy is the cleverest man the Creator ever made."

"Paddy," he would say, "is the cleverest man the Creator ever made. Mony a yin tried to steal our country and failed. The Romans tried it, so did the Danes; and we gied the English their breakfast at Bannockburn. They a' made a great mistake: they tried to take it by force. Paddy came in wi' his hat in his hand, an' *he's ta'en the country*: we canna get the use o' oor ain gallows for him."

My first promotion in this shop came to me through the other resolution, "not to lose time." We had had our St. James' Day Fair, and when the gate was opened for work, I was there. A certain man was wanted to go to Ireland, but he was not done with the Fair. They waited a day or two, but could not get him: so I was sent as a do-no-better. The job from first to last took about eighteen months. My wages were raised from the proverbial 22s. a week to 26s., and 9s. extra for being gaffer at a distance.

"The Maiden City" (Derry) was now the scene of operations. I was to see after the ironwork of a new gaswork. When I arrived I called first at the old works in Foyle Street. One old labourer, who was a little curious, said—

"Are ye come to put up the new works?"

"Yes."

"Man, man, ye're a wee bit crittur."

I met a great many likeable people here, and had some evidence of their native wit. I was one day in the smith's shop, when the tinsmith came in, and put off his coat. The blacksmith shouted—

"Aha! Willie, ye're fined a shilling."

"What for?" said Willie.

"You've on a new shirt, sir, and did not give notice."

"Sure an' it's blind ye are," said Willie, "for the owld one gave three months' notice."

Another day I was going to see the manager, and met the smith at the door.

" Are ye going in to that office, Mr. Taylor ? "

" I am, John."

" Man, they're the civilest people in the world in

"Are ye going in to that office, Mr. Taylor?"

that office; you've nuthin' more ado than ax for anything ye want, and then come away without it."

I was greatly astonished at the wages of labouring

NED FARREN AND HIS OWLD HORSE

men in this town; they had 9s. a week, masons' labourers 10s. I paid 11s., and got the pick of Derry.

When the bulk of the material was ready to come on, the firm wrote to me to call upon two or three respectable contractors, and get a price per ton for carting the iron from the quay to the works. I wrote that evening that I had done so, and that the largest contractors wanted 1s. 6d. per ton; but that there was another man, minus the respectability, who offered to do it for 10d. They said, "Engage the man at 10d." This was Ned Farren; and among all I met in Derry there is none I would like more to see again than poor Ned. He was the most good-natured, grotesque man I ever met. How he got into his coat was a mystery; and the "owld horse," as he called it, was as queer a rig-up as himself. Poor soul! I don't believe the work paid either him or his horse. I almost feel sorry I did not ask him to charge a little more; but it was my duty to study my employer's interest. While we got the work out of Ned, we all made sport of him. But I had an experience of Ned early one morning which fell like a censure on me. We were like to be stopped for want of material; I went to the quay about half-past five with the intention of stopping the men if no goods had come. I was glad to see a delivery, a boat having arrived during the night. I went straight to Ned's house, and roused him. He came to the door in Eden costume. I was shocked, but told him my message.

Ned Farren and the "owld horse."

"All roight, Mr. Taylor, I'll just *put on me*, and be round wid the owld horse in foive minutes."

I looked at the retreating figure in the passageway. "That is not the scarecrow that I am accustomed to see," said I. Lithe and handsome he was, and sweet and clean; and, if he had only had wings, would have passed for an angel. Ned was never the same to me after that. Oh, how we have insulted the Almighty by trying to adorn His handiwork.

To beguile the time in the evening, we bought a rowing-boat, four of us taking equal shares in it. The boat was only building when we bought it; so we had a ceremony at the launch, and christened it the *Spurtle*. This name aroused the curiosity of the Irishmen, but we kept the secret well. At last, one fellow came to the conclusion that it must be something Scotch, and set off to interview M'Neil of the Scotch boats.

"Mr. M'Neil, can you tell me what spurtle means?"

"Spurtle," says M'Neil, "spurtle is the pot-stick."

We adjourned after the launch to Mikey MacLaughlin's to have a social. I mention this to show the absurd notion of honourable conduct in Irish drinking. The first man to enter the house, was a labourer, who cried, "A round for this company, Mikey." The cost of the round was a third of the man's weekly wage at one swoop, and any one who retired without standing a round, was considered mean. If you sat out the orgie, you would be expected to drink some fourteen times. The party was unexpectedly broken up by the entrance of a lot of corner-boys; they were all strangers to me, but one who knew them gave me a hint of their object, and said, "I'm off." I also believed in the better part of valour, and went with him.

There was an addition to our family, while I was in Derry. My absence at such a time, was a sore trial to the mother, and an equally trying time for me. It only affords another instance of the hardness of the workman's lot. "A wife, a mother, and a slave," as I once heard a workman remark. I pity the woman who does not get sympathy from her husband. There was no lack of sympathy in our house when I was near; indeed, I took a delight in all household work. I could dress, strip, and bath a baby as well as any mid-wife in the parish; with a jug of sweet milk, I might have set up as a wet-nurse. The Scotchman I lodged with in Derry, once said to me: "It's a funny thing that none of my children will sleep with me."

I replied, "It's not funny at all. I never see you nurse or comfort your children, but I often see them entertaining you. The moment they are in trouble, you run with them to the mother as if they were burning you; no wonder none of them will sleep with you: mine would fight for the privilege."

When the latest arrival was five weeks old, the

mother brought her and our first-born to Derry, the second boy going to his grandfather for a time. The two children and the mother came cabin, a luxury the father had never yet enjoyed; deck-passage was all the firm allowed, and I say it is positively cruel to send a workman to Derry in such a manner; but there is a lot of vitality in a fellow of eight-and-twenty. The words of our national poet are applicable to many a one of them:—

> "He'll hae misfortunes great an' sma',
> But aye a heart aboon them a'."

We lived two or three months in Derry, then I was sent to Tradeston Gas Works, Glasgow, to erect the columns of two gas-holders of one hundred and twenty feet diameter. I then returned for some time to Ireland.

As I was at Londonderry several times, a great friendship sprang up between Mr. Ross, foreman, and myself. He asked me to stay at his house, Waterside, which I did. I was astonished to find that his house was not very well furnished. When he left Sunderland to come to Derry, he sold off all his furniture, and one of the reasons was he could not please his wife and his mother as to what articles he should dispense with. His mother had a grandfather's clock, and so had his wife. When he proposed to sell the mother's, the old lady dissolved in tears, and to comfort her, he said he would sell the wife's; but as this only produced a similar result with the wife, he determined to sell the whole kit.

"I am up to them now," he would say to me. "I take no more notice of the one than of the other: when a button is awanting on a garment, I give it to neither; I just open the door and pitch it in, and let them settle themselves who shall do me a service."

His courtship had a bit of romance. He was a native of Edinburgh, and after serving his time with Milne & Son, gas engineers, he had gone to Dundee. He had given in his warning, and was returning to Edinburgh in a fortnight, when he met his future wife at an evening service in church; asked if he might see her home, and was permitted. Before leaving her, he made an appointment to meet her on a certain evening at a certain corner. He was working for his employers at Baxter's Mill on the day of the appointment. At 6 P.M. he made to leave, but was told it was impossible, as the work was urgent, and he would have to work all night. Sandy would not do it; his own master could not persuade him, and said so to one of the Baxters. The latter came to Sandy, and seemed to make as little impression.

HOW HE POPPED THE QUESTION 135

Mr. Baxter being a kindly gentleman, and possessed of tact, said: "You might tell me the reason, and if it is sufficient, I will not insist."

"Hae ye ony objection to mak' my parritch."

Sandy told him the whole story, finishing up with, "What will she think of me?"

"Well," said Mr. Baxter, "I respect you for the stand you have made; but go on with your work, and I will go and meet her, and explain your absence;" *and he did.*

The next time Sandy saw his sweetheart, he said to her, "Lizzie, ye ken I'm leaving; would ye answer ae question before I go, and that is, hae ye ony objection to mak' my parritch?"

"Nane whatever, Sandy," she replied, "if ye promise to buy the meal."

CHAPTER VIII

OVER THE ALPS IN A DILIGENCE TO GENOA—SMUGGLED BOLTS—ANTONIO DANERE EX-ORGAN-GRINDER AND INTERPRETER—THE BURIAL OF THE SLATE—TAM M'GUIRE IN THE HOSPITAL—MR. WILTON—HOME AGAIN

"Where'er I roam, whatever realms I see,
My heart, untravelled, fondly turns to thee."
—*Goldsmith.*

IN 1865, I was sent to Genoa to make an extension of the gasworks at Bisango. This was a novelty: I was to see London and Paris, and actually cross the Alps at Mont Cenis. I had some care on that journey. It was a long railway ride from Paris to Saint Michel at the foot of Mont Cenis, French side. We started in the diligence late in the afternoon, and crossed the mountain in eleven hours: twenty-five minutes in the tunnel now suffices to do the journey with every manner of comfort. We stopped at station after station on the ascent to add more mules, till we had twenty-two of these beasts yoked.

What with the jingling of their bells, the shouts of the driver, and the jolting of the machine, sleep was impossible, though we were all wearied enough. The descent to the Italian side is very steep, the road winding down the mountain in a very picturesque manner. We were glad to reach Susa, where we joined the train to Turin; from the latter place we proceeded to Genoa, and put up at the English hotel till we could arrange matters. I remember when we retired to our bed-room, the apprentice who came with me said—

" By George! they have forgotten to put blankets on the bed."

" So they have," said I.

But we were so blate we did not like to complain, and agreed to try it first. We were not long down till we found the sheet was abundance; as we had been forty-eight hours without rest, we slept sound, and were awaked by many strange cries.

I called on the chief engineer of the Continental Union Gas Company, who gave me a kindly welcome. He brought out the contract for the work, laying great stress on the penalty clause, which stated that so many pounds a day would be forfeited for each and every day the work was delayed beyond the 18th of August.

"This is the 18th of August," I said.

"Yes," said he; "but if you have the new holder ready by Christmas, we will not exact the penalty; but if not, your Company shall pay for it."

We had also an iron roof to put on the retort-house. The material for the roof had arrived, so we started. I found that a lot of bolts for this had not come; and Mr. Wilton, the chief engineer, asked me what I intended to do.

"I'll take on Italian blacksmiths and make them."

"I'll not have Italian-made bolts," he said.

I heard of a firm of engineers in the neighbouring town. I went to these people, and was delighted to find they were Scotch (acclimatised).

"Man, I have the verra thing for ye," said one of them, "and as I smuggled them through in the inside of a boiler, I'll gie ye them cheap."

I wanted to know the price, but the invoice could not be found. As the man had fairly won my heart, I took them and started work at a trot. When I came to settle with the firm, we did not part such good friends. I was grievously overcharged and refused to pay, and we had an awful row. Latterly one of them said—

"Man, what are you making such a work about?

We have all been in situations like yours. I'll take twenty per cent. off, and give it to you."

Said I, "You'll take twenty per cent. off and write it on the account;" which he did, and gently hinted that if any odd things were left over when our work was done, he would buy them. I never saw him more.

When we got fair away with the work, I was sorely in need of an interpreter. Mr. Wilton said—"We have a man in our work in Sam-pier d'Arena; I will send him to you."

And he was a find. His name was Antonio Danere. He had been an organ-grinder in England. An Italian got him away from his mother when he was a mere child for a small payment, and for three years he lived with this man, going all round the country turning the handle, never learning any of the language. The treatment he received from his master was most brutal. He had also bitter memories of the English boys, who often made his

Antonio spoke English like a gentleman.

life miserable. At last he ran away from his master, and found work in some mine, I forget where. After staying seven years among the miners, he went to the Italian consul and said he wanted home to serve his time in the army; and was sent accordingly. Antonio spoke English like a gentleman. The only point on which we differed was that I had no sympathy with his saints'-days, which were too numerous for my taste. Antonio was religious, and my motto was " work, work." I did that man an injustice; I did not pay him as he ought to have been paid, considering the help he was to me with the language. The cause was a parsimonious study of the masters' interests. I never knew indeed what it was to receive a decent wage myself. I live in hopes of being in Genoa again, and if I can find Antonio, I'll pay him yet.

When the men I had hired on the spot had worked their first week, I asked the foreman at the works to make up the pays till I got better acquainted with the Italian money, which he did. I saw from the men's looks that they were not satisfied, and asked the foreman to come out and investigate. The cause was soon discovered. He had paid them at the same rate per hour as he had paid similar men in the gasworks. But we stopped work at two P.M. on Saturday, and his men stopped at three on Sunday.

"That's soon mended," I said; "give them as much for six days as you pay for seven."

And the men from that day enjoyed and appreciated some of the blessings of our country.

When the work was fairly started, some men arrived who had been engaged at another job in France. After the novelty of the place had worn off, we all found the time hang heavy on our hands. So some of us started an arithmetic class, and sat together and did sums in the meter-house. One of our number continued a week or two, but, getting tired of it, he came no more. The others resolved on a practical joke of a mild kind. They took his slate and drew a tombstone on it, and wrote: "Sacred to the memory of Jamie So-and-so, who departed this life on such and such a date." A grave was dug, and the slate was carried on spokes (the departed looking on). Tam M'Guire was chief mourner, and had long streaming bands on his bonnet made from the white cotton cloth we used for jointing the gas-holder sheets. His appearance was side-splitting. They wended their way to the grave and buried the slate, and all except one started the afternoon in a merry mood.

THE BURIAL OF THE SLATE

It was an afternoon, however, to be remembered. I thought a judgment had fallen on us for joking about death. Before half-past three, the chief mourner had fallen off the retort-house roof, a

They wended their way to the grave and buried the slate.

distance of perhaps twenty feet, on to the paved floor below. I did not see him fall, but was at his side in a minute. He was in great pain. I felt as if all resource had deserted me, far from home as I was, and ignorant of the language. However, one of the men said, "*l' ospitale*." It was enough.

We soon had a stretcher, and Tam was carried up the marble stairs and along corridors of the same materials, to one of the most palatial institutions for the relief of suffering I had ever seen; and I probably would never have seen it, but for this misfortune. I cannot tell what were the rules of the house, but I was welcome to go any evening and see Tam. His leg was broken, and he was bruised otherwise. His limb was set, and he began to mend; he became a great favourite in the house, and gave them no end of fun. The Italian language was no difficulty to him; he simply put an *a* or an *e* on to the end of his best Scotch, and roared at the nurse's ignorance if she did not understand him. One day, when he was convalescent, a young soldier, who was nearly ready to go out, wanted Tam to dance a polka. Tam protested, crying, " Basta questa, me no rise-y, me sair leggie," and the soldier jumped back as if he had been shot. What a blessing such institutions are! This one cured our friend, and gave him back to us sound in wind and limb, without fee or reward.

I think it would be difficult to find a finer specimen of an English gentleman than Mr. Wilton. Many a time he overtook me in the streets of Genoa: he would at once stop his pair of spanking greys, and say, " Jump up, Mr. Taylor, and I'll give you a lift." I felt a little ashamed to sit in the carriage beside him, and would have clothed better if I could have afforded it; but I was indistinguishable from the ordinary mechanic in my tweed trousers, cap, and canvas jacket. The mechanic who goes abroad as gaffer at the rate of eighteen shillings a week extra, will find, like the ass that snuffed up the east wind, that he'll no get very fat on't.

Gas engineering was a new departure for me, and had I not planned hard after my day's work was over, I could not have got through with credit. The gas-holder we had to build, was only 40 feet diameter, with two lifts of 25 feet each, making 50 feet in all; but the tank was so crowded round with other buildings, that we could not get sheer legs wrought upon the surface; this meant other 25 feet. Calculating 12 feet or so of clearance for blocks, slings, etc., we needed sheer legs 87 feet high. I bought four logs for the purpose, and spliced them. When we were putting them into the bottom of the tank, we knocked a brick out of its place in the top course (there was no stone cope). A busy Pecksniff of an understrapper, always ready to show Mr. Wilton the importance of having such an assistant as himself on the spot, drew his chief's attention to the brick. I was at the bottom of the tank with the men, when I heard my name called, and looking up, saw Mr. Wilton.

"Mr. Taylor," he called, "I hope you will be careful in getting on with your own work not to destroy the work of others."

He stepped back and was lost to view. I remember the feeling of rage with which I received the censure, and feel sure I swore a swear. I was up the ladder like a monkey, and away through the work in search of him.

"Mr. Wilton," I said, "I hope you do not imagine we are careless of other tradesmen's work in getting these beams into the tank. Did you ever see a place with fewer facilities for work than we have here? I feel, sir, that we are entitled to a little sympathy."

"Mr. Taylor," he said, "I have every confidence in you; it's the Italians I want you to look after."

"Well," I replied, "I don't know your experience of Italians, but I am highly pleased with them. They are as fine a lot of men as I ever had."

Wilton and I had always got on well before, and this episode did no harm. I could not attack the henchman, but it was the latter I was driving at.

We had the holder finished in plenty of time, and

about New Year I was ready to go home. Mr. Wilton said he wanted to see me before I left, so I called. He made me sit down, and read a letter he was sending by me to my firm.

"I want you to see it," he said, "before I close it."

(It was well he did so; my employer read it in my presence, and never made a remark or even smiled.) I never felt more ashamed in my life than in reading that letter, his praise of me was so lavish. He also said in the letter that he was contemplating extensive alterations in Milan the year following, and would esteem it a personal favour if I were sent back to direct them. (I was not sent.)

"Mr. Wilton," I said, "you make me feel ashamed by the praise you have given me."

"You deserve it all," he replied; and handing me an order, said, "Good-bye, and take that to the cashier."

I went to old Cerberus and got one hundred-and-twenty francs and a sneer.

I think it is Hans Christian Andersen who says, "The first moment of arrival at home is the bouquet of the whole journey." You may be sure I did not put off any time on the way. Masters need not be afraid of men trifling their time at foreign work; they are too anxious to see the old folks at home.

When I came through the old tunnel on the Glasgow and Paisley Joint Line, I was utterly intoxicated with joy; it was a feeling I know I shall never experience in this life again. I felt that the world had not lost its charm, neither had the years come when I could say, I have no pleasure in them.

CHAPTER IX

JOURNEY TO SICILY—LIFE IN THAT ISLAND—BRIGANDS—GARIBALDI—A LOYAL ORANGEMAN—A RELIGIOUS PROCESSION—A SICILIAN FUNERAL—REVOLVERS—A NOTED SCOUNDREL—HOME-COMING

> "It's no the roar on sea or shore
>   Wad mak' me langer wish to tarry,
> Nor shouts o' war that's heard afar,
>   It's leaving thee, my bonnie Mary."
>   —*Burns.*

ABOUT July, 1866, my firm wrote me to see if I would go to Sicily and put up a new work there. I said it depended on what they were prepared to offer me. I told them I could not go on the same terms as before, having made nothing by it; indeed, but for Mr. Wilton's kindness, I should have been out of pocket. They said they could not pay me more, as they had a man working on the terms proposed to me, within twenty miles of the place where I was to be sent, and that if they gave me more than he was getting, it would give rise to discontent.

"Well," said I, "I can't help it; I am not going abroad to be worse off than I am at home."

They replied: "Here is a way out of it: if you go on the old terms and hurry on the work, we will make you a handsome present when you come back."

I agreed to go. I was to take two Irishmen (labourers) with me, one to lay the gas pipes or mains for Trapani, and the other for Marsala. I had also an apprentice with me. One of the Irishmen I brought from Derry: he was a Catholic; the other was an Orangeman. I had to keep the peace between these two "boys," and generally prevent unpleasantness.

The night we left Paisley I found the Orange brother half-drunk at the railway station; he was "—— if he knew whether he was going or not," he said. He had not even the proverbial bundle in a turkey-red handkerchief. At last he agreed to go. "Four thirds for London," said I. When we got to the English capital and presented ourselves at a hotel we could not get accommodation. We tried another: it was full. I smelt a rat. The look of at least one of us was sufficient to cause a refusal. I say that it was a disgrace to the firm to send such characters to do their work abroad. No firm can indulge in the services of a lot of ne'er-do-

"Four thirds for London," said I.

weels without paying for it in one shape or another. Geordie, the Orangeman, was not a bad soul in many ways; only, he was never sober when he could help it, and his appearance was grotesque. "He came," he said, "because the boys in the shop declared it would be a nice trip, and that he would cross the Alps." In the Channel we got an awful shaking, and when we got ashore at Boulogne, Geordie said, "Thank God, Pate, we're across them Alps in safety." It had been our intention to go to Marseilles and get a boat for Palermo, but we learned that the former was declared a cholera port. So I changed the route to avoid quarantine, and struck out for Genoa. I called at the gas office, and found that Genoa was also proclaimed. We therefore hired a carriage and pair, drove to Spezzia, got rail to Pisa, took a couple of hours to see the Leaning Tower, and then to Leghorn. We got a steamer at once, on which two Greenock fellows were engineers. You need no introduction when you meet a brother Scot so far from home, and I was much in their society crossing to Palermo. The meals served on the boat were most sumptuous; I am sure the dinner would have about a dozen courses: some of my friends laid in such a stock during the first two or three courses that they could only look on in amazement during the rest, being unable to eat more.

When we got near Palermo all eyes were watching to see if the yellow flag was to be hoisted, for that would mean quarantine. We got in without it, and great was our joy, for we had had a long *détour*. My Scotch friends told me I could not travel by road to Marsala, on account of brigands, and advised me to hire a small boat and sail. They promised to get us their own boatman, who pulled them to and from their vessel when it was in port. His name was Baptiste. It was

His name was Baptiste.

well he was recommended, for he and his mate were about as bad-looking a pair of men as I ever met. We set sail on a Saturday afternoon, and arrived about ten o'clock on Sunday morning. People who have never travelled in such a capacity as ours have no conception of the utter desolation that comes over a man when the end of such a journey is reached. You look at the bare room without a fire-place, and wonder where you will sit down. Genoa was bad enough, but there you could find good lodgings; here no such thing was to be had: the rich would not take us, and the poor could not. We had to take rooms in a hotel and our food in a restaurant. My whole extra allowance went to pay my bed-room, and I had to find my food and keep wife and children at home on the ordinary weekly wage.

There is nothing calling for special remark in the construction of the gas work. It was a small one, but as we had all the street mains to lay and the public lamps to put up, we were kept busy some months. We found the Sicilians a gay and light-hearted people. Many of them are very poor, and the condition of the women is far below that of our women at home: their lot is, indeed, pitiful; there is scarcely any work for them, and they are largely at the mercy of the sterner sex. There is a little domestic service, but that is about all they can turn to, except the making of macaroni or the knitting of cotton goods, such as sox and the like. In Sicily the women spin from the distaff, as in King Solomon's time. Many of the married men keep girls in private; and I fear, though I do not know for certain, that these latter will gravitate lower and lower. There is a foundling hospital in the town of Marsala. I had often heard of the *wheel*, but here I saw it. The wheel is a contrivance which enables any one to pass a child into the institution without being seen. It is like a small barrel on end, large enough to hold a child, and revolving on trunnions. By turning the wheel, the opening comes to the outside, and the infant is snugly placed within; the wheel is then turned half round, till the opening faces the inside of the building; at this stage the person who has brought the child can signal by ringing a bell to notify the attendant. When the child has been received, it becomes the son or daughter of the *municipality*. No doubt such a place is a blessing to the children who come when they are not wanted.

We may preach against immorality till doomsday, but the sexes will not be kept separate. The pressure of the non-entity is stronger than the resisting power of the entity, the unborn more powerful than the living. The best philanthropy we can practise is to try and bring about such social conditions as will enable those to marry who desire to do so, and make the meshes of the net of bigamy a little smaller.

A few days before my arrival, a professional gentleman had been shot dead by the brigands. He had taken coach for Palermo, to pay for a cargo of material which had come for the gas works: he had a good deal of money with him, refused to deliver—

with the result stated. I was told that well-to-do people would not tell even their wives the time of their departure on a journey. It was generally believed that some of the apparently respectable frequenters of the Casino were in league with the brigands, and sent them word when they heard of intending travellers. The brigands do not care whether a man has money or not: they hold his person to ransom, and send word to his friends that if ransom is not forthcoming by a certain day, the ears of the prisoner will be sent as a first instalment. After a murder takes place, the Government sends four mounted soldiers to escort the diligence, but after a time things are considered quiet, and the game proceeds *de nouva*.

Our party arrived in Marsala in the year 1866. As Garibaldi landed at this port in 1860 with his 1000 volunteers, we heard many stories about him, and saw and conversed with many who had joined him. I was well acquainted with the man who, on the hero's arrival, took horse and rode to Trapani with the news. The magistrates of the latter town thereupon shut the gates, not so much to keep Garibaldi out as to keep volunteers in. There was a gentleman I knew, who had married the daughter of the British consul at Palermo. He told me that shortly before Garibaldi set sail, some Neapolitan soldiers came to search the British Embassy for arms, as it was well known that British sympathy was on the side of the Revolution. The Consul objected, and the soldiers persisted.

"Well, gentlemen," said the Consul, "will you just wait a little?"

"Of course, we will wait," they said.

The Consul disappeared, but was back in a minute. Spreading the British flag in the hall, the Consul said: "Now, gentlemen, at your peril."

They looked at the old rag, and went away for further instructions. They never came back.

Geordie, whom I took to lay the gas-mains of Trapani, was the third man on the job, and *he* finished it. The two chief reasons contributing to his success were—(1) he was an Irishman, and (2) he was half-drunk all the time. The streets were narrow and the houses high; and before every house there was a cesspool into which the bye-products found their way. The poor wretch was no sooner through one cesspool than he had to encounter another; and how he lived through it is a mystery. Whited sepulchres, full of dead men's bones, would have been Paradise to what he had to face.

Geordie was a great Orangeman, and a lot of the

Scotch, English, and Maltese, who were on the job, got up a practical joke to make Geordie divulge the pass-words of the Orange Society. They asked if he would become a Freemason, and he consented. They pretended to have received a dispensation from the Grand Lodge of Palermo to make a few members, of which he might be one. They held a preliminary social, at which there was plenty of Marsala wine; and when they thought Geordie sufficiently primed, they adjourned to a room, improvised as a lodge. He was duly blind-folded and taken to the House of Mourning; from that to the Mortuary, passed into the Cemetery, and through the Resurrection Gate. He was then placed bound on a chair, called the Ascension Car. Here he was further admonished that, before passing into the pure fields of Freemasonry, it was necessary that he should be as pure mentally as he was materially; and that if he had any secrets in his mind, such as the grips and pass-words of other societies, he must give them up. A bacchanalian voice called out "Never." Great sorrow was expressed at this response. Geordie was too far advanced to go back, and in his sinful state could not proceed to the higher altitudes. The others gave him a little time to consider, warning him that if he remained obdurate, there was nothing for it but to cut his wizzen. Geordie immediately tipped up his chin and cried out, "*Cut away, ye blackguards.*"

I was astonished at the number of men we had working with us who had deep scars on their faces extending from the temple to the chin. The favourite method of paying off grudges is by slashing your enemy's face with a knife. One deplorable feature is that the people will not give evidence against one another in a court of law; they prefer to take their own revenge; and if a person is not able to do it himself, his relatives will do it for him. Feuds last for generations, and the devil drives a roaring trade.

There was a religious procession on Good Friday which deserves notice. Such processions are common all over Sicily. In many towns the principal characters are represented by images, but in Marsala they are represented by living men. I will not attempt to give a full description of the scene, but only touch some of its salient points.

In front of the company came a man carrying a banner on which these words were inscribed: "The death and passion of Jesus Christ." I may here explain that there were four different men representing our Saviour in the various stages of the

Tragedy. Following the man with the banner came one representing Christ instituting the Supper. He carried a piece of bread in his left hand. Every few yards he looked to heaven, the right hand being raised as if in benediction. He broke the bread and gave to his disciples. The next personage typified Christ in Gethsemene, and had a much sadder figure than the first. Judas, the traitor, walked a couple of yards before, and every few minutes he turned and pointed to the Saviour, whereupon the surrounding crowd made a rush as if to arrest the latter. The third individual represented Christ in the judgment hall. He turned now and again to look at Peter, who was very sad and downcast, and no wonder. The master he had denied was immediately before him, and a fellow-sinner came behind carrying in his arms a live cock. The fourth actor, the *Mystery*, as the Sicilians term him, portrayed Christ, scourged, crowned with thorns, and bearing His cross. I hope never to see a sadder sight than this man presented. He wore a mask, a perfect reproduction of the face of Christ, as we know it. His dress was somewhat the same as that adopted by Sir Noel Paton in his picture of *Lux in Tenebris:* the body was well bent forward, and an apparently heavy cross lay on the shoulder and along the back;

the pace was slow, and the person seemed in agony. Altogether, the picture was so realistic that I was sick for several days.

Following the Mystery was Saint Veronica, with her outspread handkerchief, on which were stamped the features of Christ. Behind her came the executioners, bold, full of importance, carrying ladders and trays with hammers and nails; and, last of all, the centurion, riding a magnificent black charger and accompanied by a retinue of Roman soldiers. Not a word was spoken; all moved along with solemn and dignified pace.

I speak neither for nor against such displays, but this one made a great impression on me, and although it is thirty-six years since then, I still feel I have seen the " despised and rejected of men."

Another feature of life at Marsala struck me as alike pleasant and odd. Every Friday, at three o'clock in the afternoon, the convent bell was tolled to remind us of the death of Christ. At the sound every workman at once doffed his cap, murmured a *benedicite*, and resumed his work again. When one considers the countries aud continents acknowledging the Christian faith and owning allegiance to the Carpenter of Nazareth, the great question first propounded on the Sea of Galilee, *What manner of man is this?* comes home to the heart and the intelligence with forceful significance.

I was invited to a funeral, and went; it was a fine opportunity to see their mode of burial. The procession was a very solemn one, with some music. I was awfully surprised when we came within what I took to be the burying-ground, to see a man come forward and, taking the coffin in his arms, stand it on end against the wall: as it bumped slightly on the stone-work, I could hear it was empty. The mourners at once turned and went back to town. I was told the body had been conveyed privately some days before, and was undergoing some preparation before being put in the coffin. Many are coffined in full dress, and a glass panel left in the lid so that relatives can see the faces of the dead long after they are gone. On All Saints' Day, the churches and the annexes are thronged with people visiting for this purpose. In buildings attached to some of the churches, you can see hundreds of skeletons pinned against the wall. It is a gruesome sight.

I had heard so much about the danger of working among the Sicilians that, to be like others, I bought a revolver and took out a licence. I carried it a few weeks, and then put it off. An old fat blacksmith I

REVOLVERS

kept, a veritable Falstaff of a man, observing that the weapon was gone, said:

"Bravo! Don Pietro, galant uomini non ha bisogna revolvere" (Good men have no need of revolvers).

My opinion is that one is safer without them. I got on very well with the people, and made many friends; and when at last I had to leave, a great number accompanied me to the small boat which was to take me to the steamer. Our parting reminded me of the parting of Paul from the elders of Ephesus; they kissed me over and over again as if I had been another Annie "amang the riggs o' barley."

I bought a revolver.

Although there were many in Marsala to whom I was sincerely attached, there were also some noted scoundrels in the place, men who could commit murder for a consideration. I did what was considered a rash and dangerous thing with one of these men who hailed from Palermo. While the excavations were going on, we had employed about fifty little boys from nine to twelve years of age. These lads were a great source of interest and fun to me. They carried away the earth, but not by means of wheelbarrows. Each of the youngsters had a mat, somewhat like those that figs come in, and which held little more than a shovelful of earth. When the mat was filled, a man placed it on the boy's head, and off the little fellow marched. They were like a regiment of ants, and it was marvellous what they did in a day. The man in charge had a pocketful of peas, and when a boy pleased him he gave him some. We had a big slouching fellow in the place whom I never liked; one day I learned that at the breakfast hour he had been acting disgracefully before all the boys. I went straight to the foreman and said, " Put that man out." The foreman was inclined to parley. " Put him out, out with him," I said; and I saw him out. I did not know it at the time, but I learned afterwards that the foreman instructed the smartest man we had (Stephano, he was called) never to let me go out of the work without seeing me past this man's door, and to wait till I came back from town and see me in again. The fellow never disturbed me; he was an unmitigated scoundrel, and a tout for his own wife.

HOME-COMING

While I was much touched with my leave-taking at Marsala, I was truly thankful to get away. I would not have settled in the place for any money, and now all my hopes of bettering myself were blasted, as I bitterly knew from my account. I was £7 short; my wardrobe was used up; I was as poor as the Irish woman who said she had not as much as would cushion a crutch. I got a steamer at Palermo for Genoa, took train at Genoa and travelled straight to Paisley without a break—over the Alps again in a diligence, and through Paris while the great Exhibition of 1867 was on. I had no money to spend on exhibitions, and was in a hurry to see Jim, who had been born in my absence, and was now seven months old.

I had an interview with my employers, and let them know how dispirited I was; but they gave me the *handsome present* promised—£10. I was, as I said, £7 out of pocket; so with the remaining £3 I bought a tweed suit, lest I should be arrested for a rogue and a vagabond.

CHAPTER X

Off to Galashiels—The Traveller's Rest—Free Library—I become a member of the School Board—Death in the house—Steel springs—The Highland fling—My first cheque—A co-partnery—A children's church

"Although his daddie was nae laird,
   And though I hae na mickle tocher;
Yet rich in kindest, truest love,
   We'll tent our flocks on Gala Water."
—*Burns.*

"It's dowie at the hint o' hairst,
   At the wa' gang o' the swallow;
When the win's are cauld, and the burns are bauld,
   An' the wuds are hingin' yellow.

"But, Oh! it's dowier far to see
   The wa' gang of ane the heart gangs wi',
The dead-set o' a shining e'e,
   That darkens the weary world on thee."
—*H. Ainslie.*

In a few weeks, I was sent off to Galashiels, to put up a gas-holder tank. I had tried hard to get another situation, and only went to Gala at the point of the bayonet. Cheer up! lads who may be similarly placed: you never know when or where the Good Lord is going to bless you.

By and by, I brought my wife and children through to Gala, that I might have a little of their society. When my wife and four children stepped out of the train, a porter asked if all the children were twins.

Going home one night to our lodgings, I saw a notice in a stationer's window that an engineer was wanted for one of the mills in town. I told my wife, and we consulted our landlady, who cried, "Oh! *Grand Maisters*; and they call the mill the *Traveller's Rest*." I went off at once to see them, and had a pleasant interview; they would have engaged me on the spot, but I asked a night to consider it. I went back next day, and took the job at a wage of twenty-eight shillings a week. I promised to come as soon as my firm could send a man to relieve me. The master himself came through from Paisley, bringing my successor with him. I parted from his firm, after five years' service, a sadder and wiser man, richer in one point, and only in one, viz., experience.

I never enjoyed any place better than the Traveller's Rest. The masters were *gentlemen*, and I got on well with them. I was allowed to plan and execute many things, and the work was a never-ending delight. The mill was large, and some of the machinery greatly neglected. I had so much overtime that my pay was never under £2 a week. My reputation also rose quickly, at which I laughed in my own sleeve. The Jacquard machines on the looms were fearfully out of order. I took one down, to see what could be done. It was coated with hardened oil, a quarter of an inch thick and more. I put the saw through a large oil-barrel and made two good tubs. Into one of them I put twenty pails of hot water and a bucket of soda, and taking the *witch*, as they called the Jacquard, I put her in to steep. She came out rejuvenated; where a pin was worn, I replaced it, and where a hole was wide, I bushed it. In a few days I set her to work again. The master came in, in high glee, to see when I could do the other ninety-six. I said that it was not an engineer that was needed in the work, but the Wizard of the North. We could not get the Wizard, so we got more mechanics, and the work went on apace.

Hawick advertised for a gas manager, and I applied. I told our carding-master so.

"Oh," he said, "I hope the masters won't hear of it."

"Why?" I asked.

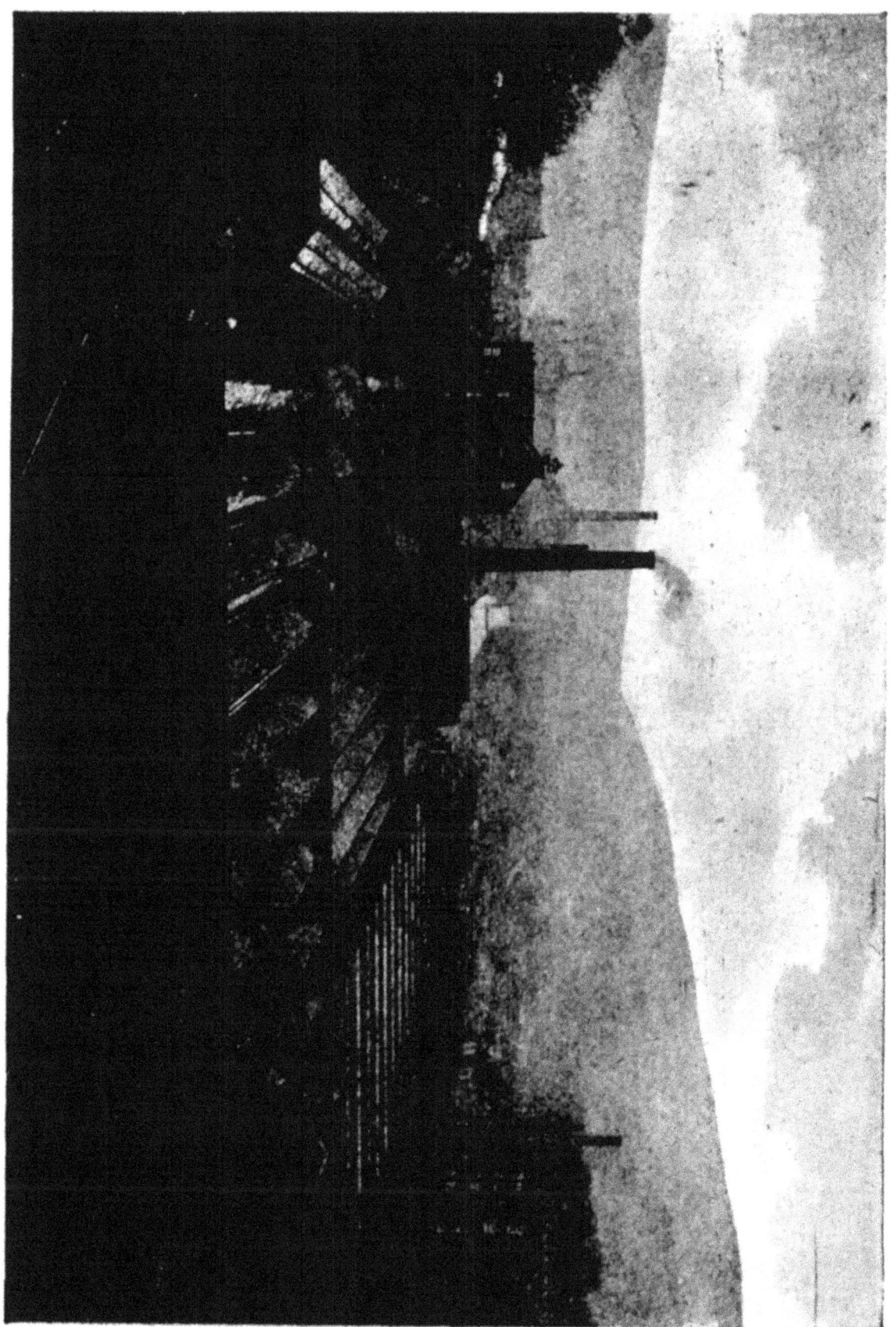

"The Traveller's Rest" Galashiels.—Page 168.

Free Library, Galashiels.—Page 169.

"I doubt they wadna be pleased."

"Well," I said, "I'll tell them."

I wanted a day at anyrate to go and see the directors, so I told Mr. Robert, and he gave me liberty. Next day, he came and asked me how I got on. He said:

"We are very well pleased with you, and whether you get the job or not, we are going to give you an advance of two shillings and sixpence per week."

I did not get to Hawick, thank God. By and bye, I got other advances, till I had thirty-five shillings a week. I learned a great deal in this mill. My experience before had been engines, locomotive and marine, and, of course, the gas plant referred to; here, I was in the midst of textile machinery. As I stood and looked at the life-like and intelligent movement of the self-acting mule, there was moisture in my eyes.

I touched the public life of the town a little, joined the Mechanics' Institute, and gave it a new lease of life. A meeting was called for the purpose of considering the advisability of winding it up. Mr. Richard Lees was in the chair. I pled for another trial, and got a number of working-men in the various mills to take an interest in it. The annual course of lectures was indeed a feature of the town. Dr. Gloag had just come to the Parish Church, and we secured him to give the opening lecture: his subject was "Free Libraries." He hit the nail on the head, and the very nail we wanted. We called a meeting at once, while the subject was fresh. I drafted the first resolution before going to the meeting, lest no other one should be prepared. It was as well, for no one else had any plan. The resolution was mild, proposing merely to obtain information from other towns where free libraries existed, and report. In this way we kept the matter simmering, and by our next meeting the thing was fairly launched. The manufacturers took the matter up, and subscribed £1800. Then the town was canvassed, and a few hundreds more got. I was made secretary, and the result was the Free Library, which has been such a boon to the town.

A member of the first School Board having refused to take office, the obligation rested with the Board to fill the vacancy. The chairman, Mr. William Brown, of Gala Hill, called on me and persuaded me to go in, in the working-men's interest, which I did.

The Good Templar movement was also in full swing, and many notable characters were reformed through its means. I thought it right to cast in my lot with the good cause, and give it a shove. I still hold total abstinence principles, my only regret being that I did not hold them earlier.

Our fifth child, Jeanie, was born 2nd May, 1869. She lived only a few months, but long enough to twine herself about our hearts. We saw she was not strong, and it only doubled our love and attention. The last night she lived, my wife and I agreed to divide the watch. I got Maggie to lie down first; the baby was in the cradle, and I kept guard. At midnight the child took some nervous twitching, which distorted the sweet little face. I was greatly frightened, awoke Maggie, and reported. In a house like ours it was difficult to carry out the Scripture injunction—" And thou when thou prayest *enter into thy closet,* etc." When Maggie rose, she went at once and opened a *press door*, and I knew fine she was praying behind the shelter of it. I am glad to say the child never took another of the turns, but slept peacefully away, with no witnesses but her father and mother.

In this same house our boy, Jim, also took trouble, in the knee. This alarmed us, and the boy grew worse and worse. The local doctor sent me with the boy to Edinburgh Infirmary to consult a professor. As I carried Jim through the quadrangle and read these words on the face of the building, "I was sick and ye visited me," he wondered what was vexing me. The old professor and his students looked at the boy and then whispered among themselves. "I'll write to your doctor," said the professor at length. This remark greatly disappointed me, for our doctor had little to say about the wee fellow. What I wanted was good news if possible, or at least information. I could not help thinking that if my social position had been better, the answer would have been different. There was a *hallicat* student who lingered behind the others, and hurriedly whispered to me, "It's a bad case." I felt grateful to the lad even for that. There was nothing for it but to bring the boy back to the taciturnity of the home doctor. But if I had been worth a £10 note, I would have asked his bill quick. Although he attended the child more than a year, he never won his confidence; the wee fellow's countenance fell the moment he appeared. One day he brought another doctor for a consultation, and when they had gone Jim said to me: "Father, could you not get *Dr. Ma-Dougall*." The latter carried the citadel at one visit. I spoke to the doctor several times about taking the limb off. He answered me haughtily, "I'll tell you when its time for that." Well, to that it came. I told Jim one day at breakfast-time that I was going to stay all day with him. He was so glad; I was playing with him and keeping him cheery, while my heart was like to break, awaiting the coming of four doctors. The operation was successful and the boy was mending, when it was discovered that the other limb was useless and somewhat out of place, owing to his having lain so long in one position. The doctor was alarmed, and I saw it. As soon as possible he gave the child chloroform, and, taking him by the ankle, made the whole limb play at the knee and the hip joints in a manner fearful to behold. The child almost died under the anæsthetic, and the windows were thrown open in a hurry. However, he came out of it, but survived only one day; he died in my arms perfectly conscious. I told him he was dying, and asked him if he was afraid, and he answered no. The last promise he made me was to come and meet me when I go home, and I am expecting him. He was five years and four months old, and had as clear a conception of the way of salvation as any doctor of divinity in the kingdom. My poor wife, who had stood by him such a length of time by night and day, was so broken down with grief and hard work that she could not stand upright, but looked old and bowed.

Time, the great healer and consoler, brought some relief. We had much to be thankful for, and could gratefully say with old Rutherford—

" Aye the dews of sorrow were lustred with His love."

I at once returned to a small invention which had been interrupted by Jim's illness. Certain small springs were used in the mill in considerable quantities. We could not get these articles of good quality, and besides they were very dear. I thought I could make them better, and attempted to make a machine for that purpose. It was only half a success; but it showed me where the defect lay, and I began again. I shall never forget the evening when we were ready for a trial—I say *we*, for my wife was always hand and glove in all my undertakings. The children were all in bed. I sat waiting till 9 P.M., when I was to start and work till 10 to test the capacity of the tool. On the stroke I started and on the stroke I stopped, and Maggie and I counted the slain. When we found I had earned 10s. in sixty minutes (although I was an elder in a U.P. Kirk), I did not ring the bell that night as I should have done for family prayers—no! I jumped up and danced a step of the " Highland Fling."

After I had got the little springs finished, I gave some of them to the mill-manager, and they were pronounced a success. He drew the master's attention to them, and *he* came and said: "Peter, you have been making some springs, and must be out of pocket; go to the cashier and get your expenses."

I knew matters had come to a crucial point, and with much trepidation said: "Mr. Sanderson, I would like to keep this to myself. There is hardly a foreman in the mill whose wife I have not seen coming here for work. I would not like to see mine doing so, but I need the money as much as they do. As for these springs, my wife could make them at home."

I had the courage to say that much because I had made many other improvements equally profitable to them.

"Oh, very well," he said, "you are quite welcome; and if you can sell any to the neighbouring mills, do so."

Here was a concession larger than I expected; that it was more than I was entitled to, I will not say; but this I know, many a one would have taken an early opportunity of paying me off. You must not think of yourself when serving some folks in this world, but there are many good people in it for a' that.

The little industry flourished apace; I let nobody know the secret, and we worked away and got up stock. One Fast Day I went to call on some of the mills in Selkirk. What fear, and trembling, and shame I experienced! I felt as humiliated as if I had started to sell matches. I called at a mill near the station. One of the masters, a big, sharp man, said to me when I had showed my goods and told my story:

"Where's your place of business?"

"I have no place of business, sir."

"Well, what else do you do?"

"I am mechanic in the Traveller's Rest."

"You are what? Do you mean to tell me you are another's servant, and yet go about to do business of your own?"

He rubbed it in so tightly that my blood got up, and when that takes place the devil himself could not frighten me. So I went back a step to lessen the angle between our eyes, and said:

"Yes, and if my employers are satisfied, who has a right to complain?"

"Oh," he replied, "I know the Messrs. Sanderson

well, and if that is so, it's all right;" and he gave me an order.

I next went to Messrs. Waddel and Turnbull. I shall never forget the sympathetic interview I had with Mr. Waddel. He slapped me on the shoulder, and said he was delighted to see new industries taking root in the neighbourhood, and told me to stick in. I came home in good spirits. An order soon came from a firm in Hawick for £28 worth, and took all our stock. By and bye the cheque came, and I went to the bank at the dinner hour to cash it. It was the first cheque I had handled. The teller took some suspicious glances at me, examined the cheque, and looked at me again. He handed me the money; and to show him I was no rogue, I took plenty of time and counted it twice. You bet I was a proud man all the same. I called on the doctor that night, and squared his bill, which I thought very moderate.

Having got hold of a little business which was new to Scotland, I thought I could not do better than bring it to the old town I love so well. I told my masters so; they were sorry, and so was I. They made me a very generous offer, but my plans were made and it was well I left. Though thirty years have passed since then, I am still in touch with my old masters in the "Traveller's Rest." I formed a co-partnery with my brothers; our united capital was £120. Co-partnery in business is like marriage in life; if it is good, it brings the maximum of b'essing—and that was our experience. My brothers took charge of the commercial side, and I had only to produce. Like Kate Dalrymple, we were eident and thrifty. In 1898, the value of our works, stock, and plant stood about £30,000.

While busy all the week with our ever-extending business, I was also busy on Sundays for others. And yet it was not altogether for others, for you cannot work for others without being blessed yourself. My wife and I had a Children's Church for nearly twenty-four years. We used the Glasgow Foundry Boys' Text-book all the time. I am fain to acknowledge the great service done by this society in issuing such a book for the benefit of those engaged in teaching. Without a book of the kind, half one's time would be lost in searching for a suitable subject; in the text-book I refer to, everything is ready to hand—the text and the Bible reading are so admirably suited that the teacher can get to work at once. I have nothing to say against commentators, but they were never of much service to me. An intimate knowledge of Scripture, such as one can get by using good old crazy Cruden and

Dr. Eadie's *Biblical Encyclopædia*, together with the reflection of one passage upon another, were the foundations upon which my work was built. I had a busy and happy time at these meetings, and few Sunday nights passed that I did not speak at some mission gathering in my own rough-and-tumble style.

Many years ago our firm resolved to open offices in England, as the greater part of our trade was there; and so at that time I had much travelling between Paisley and the South. I used to go second-class for the privacy, and generally got some new ideas on the way. One day I had taken my seat in the train at Glasgow, but saw I was to have a companion who was standing at the door speaking to another gentleman who was seeing him off.

"Noo, Jackson," said his friend, "be sure and send me the drawings o' thae pumps." And Jackson promised and the train started off.

After a bit I said, "Do you object to smoking?"

"Oh, no," he replied, "I smoke myself, but not much."

We got into conversation; I found he was an engine-driver on the L. & N.-W. Railway, and had been down with some special engines of the Company's making for the Highland Railway. We had a very interesting time of it: he knew every yard of the line, and as we drew near the place where we were to part, he asked if I had ever seen the Company's works at Crewe. I said no: I had passed the station but never been ashore. I had only known one lad that had gone there some twenty-five years ago, called Charlie Dick.

"Dick, Dick, Dick," he said; "why, that's the name of our manager."

I smiled: "It's too good to be my Dick. Is he a Scotchman?"

"Yes."

"Does he belong to Dundee?"

"I could not answer that."

"Well, what like is he?"

"He's very like yourself."

I tore a leaf out of my note-book and wrote: "If you are my old bed-fellow at 'The World's End,' write to me at once." I gave this to Jackson and we parted. I waited two days and no word came. I then wrote a very humble apology to the manager of Crewe Works. But I got a long letter in reply, and who was the manager but just my old friend, the Christian Philosopher, who went in alone and took the place step by step till he had six thousand men under him. I shall transcribe his letter in the next chapter.

Charlie Dick.—Page 181.

CHAPTER XI

Two letters from Crewe

" Friend after friend departs,
  Who hath not lost a friend?
There is no union here of hearts
  That hath not here an end."

"Deva Villa,
"Crewe, September 23, 1886.

" My Dear Old Friend,

"I was very pleased indeed to get your note by Jackson, also that of the 10th. I am ashamed that I have not replied sooner, but I am a very, very bad correspondent, whether from natural indolence or acquired laziness, I will not discuss at present; but this I know, that it requires a good deal of pressure to get me started letter-writing. A nice confession! you will say. Well, writing or no writing, the world goes on. Often, often, have I thought of our short friendship, and wondered where you were and what you were doing; and I am glad to hear, though you have not said much, that you have prospered in the world. What are you doing? What about the family? And I hope your good wife (that greatest blessing to a man) is alive, and that true helpmeet which a good wife is. I lost my wife four years ago, and I feel the loss more every year. I have four children with me, and four have gone before. One is just twenty-one; he is in the works, and is doing fairly well. No. 2 is a junior clerk in the Goods Department of the Railway. No. 3, a boy, is at school; No. 4 is a girl, twelve years old, and also at school. I have done fairly well. I see many points where I could have done better, but I must not complain; some have done better, others not so well. I have had a hard uphill fight, and now feel I am getting an old man through it all. Write me a long letter, giving me all your history since we parted. Do you recollect the old Scotch song-book we had in the 'World's End' in Glasgow, not the place where we got tea-leaves in our porridge. I want the last line of a verse which is associated with the book and you:

> ' Oh, the mucking o' Geordie's byre,
> The shoolin' the gruip sae clean,
> Ilk dad o' the scartle strak fire.'

I want the next line, and hope you will write soon and give me full particulars of you and your belongings.

"I remain,

"Your old friend,

"C. Dick."

On October 13th I received the following letter from him :—

"Dear Peter,

"I was delighted to receive your long letter and especially to hear that after your uphill fight you are now able to take life easier. It is very gratifying to me to read such a long and pleasing account of you. I am very pleased to hear that your wife is still living: long may she be! I should have wished to receive your photo, but perhaps that will come soon. I am sorry to say that I cannot send you one: I have not had any taken for about ten years, and have no copies. I am glad to hear of your invention and that you have done so well with it. It must be grand to be your own master. Although I have done fairly well, I have not attained to that, nor could I at present think of laying by in comfort.

"Well, after we parted, I went to Liverpool, and after hanging about a week or two, I got a job in Jack's, worked for about three months, often at repairs in the docks, working late, sometimes all night. They got slack, and about fifty were turned off: I was not in the first batch but in the second or third. I then started off, intending to go to Birmingham, but was advised to try Crewe, and here I got work and here I remain. I worked for some time in the repairing shop, repairing and rebuilding engines. The works were being extended, and in about two years I was made leading hand in charge of an engine. Meantime, I attended the drawing and other classes in the Mechanics' Institute, where there was very good teaching, and so in another year I was taken into the drawing-office to assist in tracing; there were about fifteen in the office. After some years of plodding and hard work, I was appointed to take charge in the absence of the chief. In 1871 I was made chief with small pay, heavy work, and long hours. In 1877 the signal superintendent left, and I was appointed. I had charge of all the new signalling, and the maintenance of the old. This involved a lot of travelling and exposure, and I suffered severely. I designed and carried out the signalling arrangements for nearly all the large stations on the line—Willesden, Bletchley, Northampton, Stafford, Crewe, Liverpool, Holyhead, Preston, and Carlisle.

"In 1881, the manager of the works left to be loco-superintendent on the Great Eastern Railway, and I was appointed works-manager, a very heavy job. The salary is fair and I ought to be content, but it is worth as much again. You may have some idea of the size of the place when I tell you that we employ 6300 men; if there was one 0 less it would be comfortable. The works are very straggling, and cover about 90 acres; 25 acres are covered with shops and sheds. We usually have about 280 engines under, or awaiting, repairs; lately we have been building about 70 a year, but for some years we did about 110 and one year 140. But the loco. work is a very small part of the whole. We make all our own steel; all our boilers have been made of steel for many years, with the exception of the copper fire-box. We also make our own stationary boilers, and are just finishing 12 marine boilers for our marine department. We make the steel rails and even sleepers of steel, steel bridges for our permanent way department, steel carriage and waggon-axles and tyres. From the scrap we make nails. We are now casting our loco. wheels in steel without forging. Our superintendent is chief mechanical engineer for the whole system. Here we make our own warehouse cranes; hand, hydraulic, stationary, and pumping engines for all the system; besides engine and waggon turnstiles, foot bridges for stations, and wooden feet, hands, and arms for those crippled in the service. For many years we have also done our own building—that is to say, the joiner and iron work of shops and of sheds up and down the line. We make on an average 100,000 red bricks per week, and have done so for years, not to speak of drain-pipes and concrete stone. We make the gas for the works, and also supply the town—this fact will interest you, who are a gas engineer; we have been building new gas-works to make 50,000 per hour, and have just commenced this week to make the gas. Our own men and material have done everything, except a few specialities, such as centre-valve meter, exhauster and condenser. We are just finishing eight cottages adjoining, and have started building infant schools. We make iron hurdles for fencing off the rails out of old rails and other scrap. We have also washing and wringing machines and drying stoves; we wash and dry all sponge cloths used in engine cleaning, and also the oily waste for the carriage lamps. But enough of that.

"I have been a member of the Crewe Town Council for the last six years, and retire this month. I am nominated for re-election, and fondly hoped there would be no contest in my ward; but I learned yesterday that we are going to have a fight. The election is next Monday, and I will let you know the result. We have often hard fighting (wordy only) at the elections, and often rough times at the Council meetings.

"I have made a good many attempts at this letter: it is much longer than, I am used to, but I must finish; the next few nights must be devoted to electioneering. Many thanks for your invitation, but I think that with your English business you are more likely to be in this neighbourhood than I am to be in the North. I shall be very glad to see you here. If I have a chance of getting North, I will not fail to call at Paisley. With very kind regards to yourself, wife, and family.

"I am, dear Peter,

"Your old friend,

"C. Dick."

My son and I went and spent a day with Charlie at Crewe. I could see his heavy responsibilities were telling on him. I am sorry to say that he died two years after. I never saw him in the interval.

I may as well mention here what became of another character mentioned in a previous chapter. One day I was told that a gentleman wanted to see me in my office. When I saw the individual, he said : " Did ye ever see this face before ? "

There was no mistaking it ; it was one of the kind which defies time.

" You're my old friend Peter," I said, " who took the narrow way and went up the lum."

I was angry with him for never coming to see me ; he knew where to find me, but I did not know where to find him. He had been sailing the North Sea all these years as engineer, and was now retired. All the members of our youthful debating society that I can trace have prospered. M'Lean was doing well as Chief Engineer and making money, but was taken ill and died abroad many years ago. Crawford is still living, and is a Heating and Consulting Engineer in New York.

DIARY OF A TRIP TO AUSTRALIA

DIARY OF A TRIP TO AUSTRALIA
(1887-1888)

Captain Cook landed at Botany Bay, April 28th, 1770, hoisted the British flag and, in the name and right of George III., took possession of the whole eastern coast, with all its bays, harbours, and islands; fired three volleys of small arms, which were answered by the same number of volleys from the ship. The new " Possession Land," thus formally annexed, had an area of 3,000,000 square miles.

BAY OF BISCAY — GIBRALTAR — A DEATH — IRISH QUESTION—LASCARS—MALTA—RELIGION OF TO-DAY—PORT SAID—SUEZ—ADEN—FELLOW PASSENGERS—THE PAISLEY CLUB—COLOMBO—MELBOURNE NOTES—JANOLEN CAVES—ROCKYMOUTH—COLONIAL DIET—VICTORIA MINT—ROAD HOME—POETRY—EGYPT AND THE PYRAMIDS—MALTA—DISCUSSIONS ON SUNDRY TOPICS—ROYALTY AND REMINISCENCES.

November 7th, 1887.—I believe it is customary for important people, and for those who think they are so, to write some account of their travels, to astonish the old fossils who stay at home.

I am not an important man, nor do I think myself so, and my only excuse for beginning this chronicle is that my brother, who is with me, had a note-book, and we thought it a pity not to use it.

At 12.30 on Saturday, 5th November, we waved our last salute to our friends at Albert Docks, London. We cleared about 2 P.M., and had a good run to Plymouth, leaving that port about 12.30 on Sunday, the 6th. We are now ploughing our way through the Bay—the Bay of Biscay, O! We have people here who have been through it before, and they say it is as rough as they have ever seen it. Well, neither my brother nor I have been sick, which is a mercy. Last night was a sore night with many of the passengers, and also with the stewards, who were kept busy. We did not sleep, or at least it was only by snatches.

It is comical to see people walk on deck. The stewards at meal-time look so odd: you would think one leg was six inches longer than the other. Things are not in good order yet, and if they do not improve, there will be complaints.

We have a large number of passengers, and any I have spoken to are very nice.

Gazing round the cabin, at the dinner-hour, I

think the captain (Capt. Tomlin) has the finest head in the ship.

November 9th.—We have just passed Gibraltar. The day is exceedingly fine. We had a good view of the Rock, and all regretted it was impossible to land. We passed Trafalgar Bay shortly before, where Nelson gained his greatest victory. The African coast was also visible. Our vessel is going well—her run in the last twenty-four hours being 380 miles.

You would think one leg was six inches shorter than the other.

The passengers are all out of their cabins now: they seem agreeable people, but quiet. There was some singing in the second saloon last night, and I hear they are going to give a concert to-morrow night. I wonder at the colonials. They seem to be Conservative in politics; one good friend here has a perfect hatred of Gladstone. While passing Gibraltar he said he would not be astonished some day to hear that Gladstone wanted to give it up. I said: "Even if he did, would he be worse than Sir George Rooke, who stole it on July 24th, 1704?" He replied that Rooke did not steal it, but fought for it. Of course, might is right! They promise, if I stay twelve months in the colonies, I shall go home cured of my Radicalism. We shall see.

There must be some wealthy people travelling here: lots of wine and champagne going.

November 10th.—The passengers were all sorry to learn this morning that a young lady in the first saloon had died during the night. Her name was Miss Stewart. According to report, she had hurt herself with study, and was in a weak state both of body and mind. She was nineteen years of age. The service was very solemn. At twelve o'clock, the engines were stopped, and a procession was formed, headed by a Church of England clergyman, followed by the few English sailors on board carrying the body. The coffin was wrapped in the Union Jack, and the sailors' caps were placed on the top. The captain, with the chief officers and others, came behind. At the word, the coffin was committed to the deep, the plank was raised, and the girl slipped from under the shelter of the Union Jack to the keeping of Him who is the resurrection and the life. There was a plunge in the calm waters of the Mediterranean, and " the sea, the blue lone sea, had one."

The Lord's Prayer, repeated by all, and the benediction of the clergyman, made a fitting close to the sad ceremonial. " So teach us to number our days that we may apply our hearts unto wisdom ! "

November 11th.—I have had a long conversation with an Irishman on board. He is from Waterford. He thinks there is much to put right in Ireland with regard to the land, but does not approve of the means used by the Land League. He does not like the Members of Parliament (Irish). He thinks the first principle of all dealing is honesty, and that a man has the right to meet his just obligations—a doctrine with which I cordially agree. I asked him if the Irish representatives did not teach that. He said, " They do, but in such a way that the other thing is the result." He leased three farms in Ireland at one time, and had experience of three different kinds of landlords and landladies. One was in straitened circumstances, and had to *get all* and *give nothing*; another acted fair and square, and was willing to meet him in a just and friendly spirit; the third was a greedy, grasping person, without the excuse of the first.

He saw the land question was coming to the front, and sold out ten years ago. For one farm he got £800 for his interest, and if he had kept it till to-day, he would not have got *eightpence*. He objects to the coercion of the Irish people, as well as the coercion of the English Government. He says a man will come to you and say, " I have not paid my rent, and by —— if you pay yours I'll break your head." And break your head he will! He does not think the Irish people will be content even with the land question adjusted, and he would like Home Rule, if the proper people could be got to go into Parliament. He complains that such men have retired, even from municipal life: people of talent, moderation, and honesty, will not go in to be bullied by those of coarser manners; and so the standard has been lowered. Well, we are suffering from the same thing in Scotland: not that we accuse the parties in office of anything disreputable; but the moral tone is not what it might be, and duty has been shirked because disagreeable. What a man, or a people sow, that shall they also reap. I think from a remark my friend made, he must be in the spirit trade, as he says he pays £15,000 a year to the Government. He told me of an employer in his neighbourhood, called Jones, who was in the wool and skin way, with six hundred workers, and who refused to contribute to the National League Funds. He was made so uncomfortable, that he sold out and left the country. He has heard since that Jones is in business in Scotland, where, he says, he is only making half the profit he did in Ireland; the people (his workers) have the other half; but *he has peace and liberty.* Just so! It is a pity Ireland is so impoverished; perhaps if she had had the half which is now going to the Scotch, Jones would not have required to flit.

He also added: "You see, I am an Irishman. I have lived in Ireland. I would like to have a little bit of the island, say half an acre, where I could build a cottage and just say it was my own. I would most willingly pay any reasonable price for it, but I cannot get it."

I had a long talk with one of the engineers. I do not know his rank, but think he is chief. I thought they had to feed the boilers with salt water. This is not the case. They start with a stock of fresh water, and as it leaves the condenser it is put back into the boiler, and used over and over again. This could not be done formerly, but I see how it is now possible with the surface condenser.

While we were speaking, one of the Lascars, of whom there are about seventy on board as sailors, greasers, etc., came and asked him something. When the man left, I said: "How do you like these fellows?"

"Oh," he said, "I would not give one of them for a dozen Englishmen. Englishmen make a spurt about, and then go and sit down together and yarn and smoke; and when you go into port, the chances are you will not have a sober one to leave with. I have seen us," he continued, "forced to fire ourselves, while they were lying drunk in the stokehole. No, if Englishmen are not here they have themselves to blame. The Lascars are always at their post when they ought to be, and whatever is entrusted to them you can depend on having done."

My poor country! You are making up a bad record, and the day of reckoning is coming.

November 12th.—We arrived at Malta, and anchored at 8.30 A.M.

The place is very nice. We were not allowed to

land, as I hear that there is one case of cholera in the town, and so strict are the regulations that a box marked " For Colombo," which had been placed upon a barge alongside, could not be brought on board again. It must be sent to London, and start afresh on the journey.

A great deal of fun and discussion goes on in the second cabin, which is the most cheerful part of the ship. It reminds me of the difference between the House of Commons and the House of Lords. One old fellow said the day was coming when Australia would be severed from the old country, and there was a storm raised—I never heard a louder—with cries of " Never! Never! " The feeling among the colonials, to a man, seems to be that by-and-bye they shall have a representation in an Imperial Parliament, and for that they are content to wait. Home Rule they have already; when they are a little older they will get a share in the business. In the same way a father does not give his son at eighteen or twenty the same say as himself, yet it will come when the son is matured. I was glad to find this loyal and patriotic feeling, and I hope and believe it will be as they say.

We left Malta at half-past four. We had a good view of it from the ship. It seems a rocky, bare place, with only little bits of green patches. The buildings are fine and quite Eastern, with a mixture of Paisley, Athens, and Jerusalem.

November 13th.—I was having a smoke last night when a Mr. Munroe called me over to his side of the saloon, and said: "There is a gentleman here who wishes to speak to you." He turns out to be a Mr. Archibald Blair, with whom I used to run when we were at Muir's School in Seedhills, forty years ago. We called up so many old stories that though we spent the whole evening together, it was too short. He is representing the London and Lancashire Insurance Company, and no doubt has prospered well. This is his third winter of travel. He has been all over the world where men have anything to insure. His brother, John, who was delicate, is a lawyer in Edinburgh, and rich. I can scarcely find an old school companion in Paisley, and strange that I should meet one here in the neighbourhood of Malta.

Preparation has been made for divine service to-day, and a choir has been practising. I hope we shall have refreshment from the Old, Old Story. I have grave doubts about the religion of to-day—Church of England, Presbyterian, or any other you like. Men stand with a certain amount of awe and worship reverently at a distance; but when you come near to find it in their lives and principles, it is not there. And if the Lord was coming back, I will not say they would crucify Him, but they would hoot Him from one end of the ship to another. It does not suit our people of means to preach, " Thou shalt love thy neighbour as thyself." All men who have the desire to raise the mass of mankind are agitators, demagogues. Henry George is a madman. A portrait of Gladstone was tacked up in the saloon yesterday. It was a print from *Vanity Fair*, and partly a caricature. A gentleman wrote below, " The traitor who sold his country!" and another added, " The Grand Old Dog!" I do not grudge our swells their wines and brandies and whiskies and choice cigars, and ease and comfort, but when I see their contempt for the men who produce all these, and by whose skill they travel in such luxuriant security, it makes me a Shimei that can only stand and swear.

November 14th (Monday).—We had divine service yesterday in the saloon—the captain reading two chapters, and the English clergyman preaching a short and forcible sermon. The saloon was well filled, but that can only accommodate half of the passengers. Four young swells started playing cards, as is their usual, and I saw money on the table. Mr. Neilson, an old colonial, said he had been across nine times and never saw cards on Sunday before. Several people said it was offensive, but no one spoke to the young gentlemen. I do not think, however, it will be repeated; they will come to know the mind of the passengers, and public opinion is a powerful weapon. It is pitiful to see these young fellows early in the day with whiskies and sodas and cards.

The smoking-room was very lively last night. People have got acquainted, and all reserve is laid aside. Many subjects were spoken of, and men are men, and I like them. Despite all differences in politics, there is much, in social intercourse, to be admired and appreciated. Where many of them and I fall out is when we come to deal with our fellow-creatures collectively. Then, of course, they wish to be served, and, if a man is poor, they say he ought to work. They will hardly believe that there are honest people seeking work and unable to find it.

Amongst the many things needed in these days is the moral elevation of the people. If they would respect themselves more, employers would feel ashamed to offer the wages at present given. I am told by a Glasgow gentleman here, of an engineer in Glasgow in the locomotive way, whose annual income is £65,000. If society was as it should be, something less might do him; and, if the balance were to go to his workers, more money might be circulated. These immense sums lie idle, or are squandered in some bogus speculation, while gaunt human beings parade our streets, mere bones and rags.

November 16th.—Our good ship arrived at Port Said yesterday morning. That was a change of scenery! The coal barges, with hundreds of black men, were waiting for us, and to see them scrambling into our ship made us think we were sent for. The coal is put aboard here in baskets, or rather mats—the same as our joiners carry their tools in. These black fellows put in easily 100 tons an hour. Our ship took 900 tons, and we were only there from 8.30 till 4.

The ship was boarded also by all sorts of traders, selling sewed work, silk, photos., coral; and by a wizard who fooled us a good deal and took a lot of money. But he was clever. He stood right in the middle of the crowd on deck, and bamboozled us. His broken English was amusing. " Don't be frightened, Mr. Masher," he would say, as he touched a gentleman's nose and made it deliver a handful of coins. " S' you take hold of this, Mrs. Langtry," he would say to another. When he wanted information, he took out a small live rabbit and consulted it. He fooled around all the time we were in port, and left with his pockets full.

We went ashore, and a young fellow joined our company and walked before, saying: " Me show you Port Said." We took no notice of him for some time, but, thinking he might be useful, we spoke to him, at which he was much pleased. When I spoke to him he said, " This gentleman belong to Glasgow; me from Glasgow, too—my name Jamie Craig." We were much amused at Jamie. He took us to a public school, open to the street, where the children were all sitting like tailors. I was sorry to see a good number of them blind of an eye, which was due, I think, to bad usage. We also visited a mosque, and had to leave our shoes outside: there was not much to be seen. The surroundings are very dirty, and, if the weather was wet, I could not conceive of a worse place.

We returned to the ship, and started through the Canal. The sun was soon down, and we proceeded by electric light. It was a sight to watch the lamp.

The sand-flies, attracted by the light, came dashing against the glass, and flew away again, like arrows of fire. It was a pretty sight.

It is not easy to write in the smoking-room, owing to the frequent discussions. Some one has got word of a row with the unemployed in Trafalgar Square, and from that to the Irish question, is an easy transition: I can only sit and listen. I am amongst Tories, and should simply be eaten up, if I ventured to speak my mind; so I say nothing, but like the Highlandman's horse, have my own thought.

We are now in the Bitter Lakes. The day is very fine, but desert, desert, far and wide.

Mr. Neilson, whose company we all enjoy, told us to-day about an Irish cobbler in the colonies who used to thrash his wife most awfully. There was a deep ditch in front of the house, which served as general drain, and when Biddy was beset, she jumped the ditch. He could not do that, and had to go round by the bridge. When he came near her, Biddy skipped again. One day, when the cobbler saw Biddy preparing to leap out of his way a second time, he cried, " Biddy, Biddy, be a man and stan' ; " but Biddy could not see it.

Between the Bitter Lakes and Suez, great cuttings are being made to widen the Canal. I should say there are scores of camels at work. The Egyptians look a stalwart people. They have huts like our tinkers for sleeping in, and many are resting in the

"Biddy, Biddy, be a man and stan'."

shade of their own cuttings; but in another hour, at mid-day, there will be no shade. The sun is very hot to-day, and the helmet is a good protection.

November 17th.—We arrived yesterday at Suez about mid-day, but did not go ashore. Great crowds of natives, selling goods and fruit, came on board, and did considerable business. There seem to be comical fellows, go where you will. A dozen or more of boats were alongside in a twinkling, offering to take people ashore; and the boat which commanded the most attention was the one with the comical fellow. He was tall, well-built, and stout. One of the stewards told me he gets the name of " The Governor of Suez." He was

" The Governor of Suez."

a most voluble talker, and though we have a lot of boys in the ship, he kept them all in banter, to the amusement of the passengers. He would take us ashore, he said, for a shilling; he would provide donkeys for Suez, which is from two to three miles off; or would take us to Moses' Well, where, he said, the water was very dirty, but Moses had more sense than drink it.

"Good donkey, madam, good. English side-saddle. Come, see, my Lord Beaconsfield, and de Grand Ole Man. Yes, yes, and Mrs. Langtry, too. And Mrs. Cornwallis West. Yes, and Scots wha hae, wha ho, wi' Wallace bled!" He kept the whole ship in laughter. "Sh—you know the Prince of Wales, Him A1. De Grand Ole Man, him finished. Lord Salisbury—dat's de man! Yes. Very good!" And so on.

We had a ball on deck last night, but it was no great success. The passengers are just too dandified. Swallow-tails were trotted out, but the affair was cold, and I went early to bed.

I was asking Mr. Neilson, whom I have mentioned before, what was the size of the sheep farms he and his partner had. He said they had 70,000 acres; their ground measures 8 miles by 23, *i.e.*, 184 square miles. He was just a little farm lad when he went out, but he has some cash now. He was telling me he was once returning officer at an election. He left the polling clerk and a policeman in the booth with plenty of whisky, and only let their men away to vote at three o'clock. When he came back to the booth, the policeman and the clerk had quarelled about the election, and were fighting it out in the back-yard.

I said: "Did you school your men how to vote?"

"Of course we did. What the devil right had they to think who was best?"

This was said with a wink and a chuckle. I said: "Now that you have got a good slice of the country, I suppose every one should be content whether he has land or not."

"Of course," he said, "if they have none they should have had some. Hang it! It was all a scramble, and a survival of the fittest."

I rose this morning at half-past five, and saw the sun get up nearly an hour later. It was a splendid sight. The moment he appeared above the horizon, he was as bright and clear as could be. One could see the motion of the earth from watching his progress. We are in for a hot day. It is ten minutes past seven A.M., and the temperature in the smoking-room is seventy degrees.

November 18th.—I went ashore yesterday, and saw the town of Suez. The boatmen and donkey-boys are difficult to deal with, and this is so well known that many of the passengers stay in the boat. It would pay the merchants of the town to put a boat at the disposal of passengers for nothing, or at a nominal fee. But one has to pay the price agreed upon, and then be importuned for backsheesh by the principal, and later on by his servants.

The town to me seems a dirty place, and all the wares exposed are covered with flies.

We are now sailing down the Gulf of Suez. There is nothing to be seen but desert on either side. The very rocks have a strange appearance, and something of a pyramidal look.

I suppose we have seen Mount Sinai, though no one pointed it out. Greater desolation could not be seen. Nothing could live on these shores. To look at the waters here and think of the passage of the Children of Israel, one is forcibly drawn to the conclusion that a stupendous miracle was wrought, or else a great fraud was published.

November 21st.—We reached Aden about six P.M. We were sorry to be so late; still we were surrounded by small boats, and a few came on the ship to sell articles, but they were ordered off.

I was told a passenger in the second saloon gave one of the Somalese niggers a sovereign, and instead of giving him change, the nigger dived off the steamer.

November 22nd.—We had a Scotch concert in the second saloon, entitled "Twa Hours at Hame." Scotch selections on piano—"Och, hey, for Somebody," "Hielan' Laddie," "Robin Adair," "Jessie's Dream," "Jock o' Hazeldean," "Auld Lang Syne," etc., made a pleasant evening, and the Scotch faces were radiant. We had also a few selections on the bagpipes. You can scarcely go where the bagpipes are not before you.

When we came out of the second saloon there was a concert going on at the butcher's shop, with banjo and bones. There are some sweet singers among the stewards.

November 23rd.—We have some exceedingly nice people, and some on whom words would be wasted. An old man, the very make of a despot, stopped at Aden to look at a basket in a lady's hand. It was mine. He said, "What did you give for that?"

She replied: "A gentleman gave two shillings for it."

"Where is he?" he demanded, and I was singled out as the culprit.

He stepped back and surveyed me, as the essence of all stupidity, shoved the basket at me with disdain,

"What did you give for that?"

and walked away to prevent an explosion. I am glad he did not burst—for the atmosphere was overpowering enough as it was. A good friend of mine, and an old traveller, was writing in the saloon yesterday. He rose and went to his cabin for a note-book. When he came back a young lady said to him: "That seat is engaged; a lady is coming to occupy it."

"Indeed," he said, "I will be delighted to give it to the lady when she comes, but as I have been writing here for the last half-hour, I wonder when she engaged it."

"Oh," said her majesty, "that will be your ink-bottle, too, I suppose," as she pushed it away and upset it on the cover.

She made a fuss to wipe it up. He said: "Excuse me, madam, I will manage it better than you."

She said: "I'd better leave this table; you might be happier."

Mr. Neilson is walking round now with the doctor to see if he knows her name. She has become famous.

A fancy-dress ball came off in the evening. A Mrs. Robertson was "Britannia," and although quite a young woman, she seemed the mother of all. I never saw a lady with such a magnificent figure. With her helmet, trident, and Union Jack, she looked a power, like Paddy's cat. Each country was represented by some lady or gentleman: even Buffalo Bill was there with his lasso, and Captain O'Neill was a veritable Mephistopheles in his red cloak and high feathers. And he mixed well among the young, giving all a call, as the devil usually does.

At some leaping games in the second cabin a young man broke his arm.

November 25th.—There is a place on the port side of the deck called the Paisley Club, of which the principal members are Mr. Archibald Blair, my brother, and myself, but we are joined now and again by other Scotchmen, such as Mr. Smith, Glasgow; Mr. Neilson, Melbourne, formerly of Galloway; Mr. Allen, Sydney; Mr. Munroe, Brisbane, formerly of Renfrew; and our solicitor is Mr. Grant of Sydney, formerly of Cupar. All sorts of things are discussed, but when the club is more select Paisley comes in for the lion's share. In imagination we lime the mill holes, jump the Hammils, and tail the Linn. We discuss Johnnie Robin's monkey, the Hawkhead and Bauldy's Brig, the Seedhill Schule, the Old Quarry, and countless other features and incidents of the old town.

The Paisley Club.

November 27th.—We reached Colombo in the afternoon, and went ashore for some time. We had many invitations to look at jewellery, but we said *not to-day*. Some poor-looking beggars are to be seen here, and some are frightful to look at. Some of us went to the funeral of a Mr. Tuckett, who died on board. His daughter fainted at the grave. I could see from the grave-stones that many an English person is buried here. The cemetery is from three to four miles from the landing-stage. One can see how luxuriant the growth is here: bananas, cocoa-nut, and palm trees grow in abundance.

November 28th.—We sailed about one P.M. For an hour before that time the quartermasters were going about with ropes clearing out the merchants; and withal we have five intruders on board for a nine days' sail to King George's Sound, and the purser says he will make them pay.

November 29th.—I am told that no less than eight persons are with us from Colombo, against their will. Great sympathy is felt for a sergeant of the 91st Regiment. It seems when our boat started, the ladder, which was down, came in contact with a small boat, almost sinking it. Indeed, two of the occupants were thrown into the water; the others, including the sergeant, scrambled on to our landing-ladder, and are with us still. The captain was asked to stop and get them ashore, but he said he would not stop for the Prince of Wales. The poor sergeant had been sent to watch that no deserters left with the ship, and here he is away himself.

November 30th.—I have been told by one of the colonials that when a man got a grant of land in Australia he had to take possession and make certain improvements, but could not at the time of purchase be the servant of another. He often merely left his situation, went and slept a night on the ground granted, bribed the inspector to certify to the improvement he had made on the land, got the titles, and gave these to the man for whom he acted as dummy. He received a reward, and subsided into his old situation again.

December 5th.—We had a number of sports to-day. Some ladies set themselves to pick up potatoes a yard apart and ten in a row. One young lady, who ran several times, was so excited from exertion in the competition, that she suddenly fainted. I don't like to see ladies at this work—running, turning, and stooping.

> "Tattie racing's no for you,
> Bonnie lassie, O!"

December 8th.—We reached King George's Sound yesterday, and landed. The harbour is a fine one, made by Nature. The ground is very barren and sandy; there is a scrub growing, but the place will never be of much account except as a port. I saw one of the aboriginals and his wife. He said his name was Jamie King, and asked me if he looked wild.

December 10th.—We reached Adelaide at noon, and dropped anchor in Glenelg Harbour. The colour of the earth here is chocolate, and the grass is all burned up with the heat.

December 12th.—We arrived at Williamstown Pier at three in the morning, and proceeded to Melbourne by rail after breakfast.

The zoological gardens of this city contain as fine specimens of lions, tigers, and ostriches as are to be seen anywhere. There is a temperance refreshment bar in the grounds, and a house for supplying milk.

Whisky, ale, and porter don't have it all their own way here. In going round the city I have scanned the work-people closely. There is an air of health and energy and comfort about them superior to what we see at home, and yet it is difficult to say wherein it lies—it is so mixed up in the whole man.

It is easy to see that drink has not the sway it has in Britain. I went into a large public-house yesterday which has a temperance bar. You can have tea, coffee, milk, beef-tea, and eatables of all kinds. That would be too much trouble for Mr. Bung at home.

No man can look at this city, which has grown up in forty years, without mingled surprise and admiration. The streets are well laid out, and the buildings will compare with those of our own cities. The tram-car service is immensely superior to any running in England. They have cable cars, as in Chicago, which travel very fast, and will face any gradient. There are three hundred such cars at work. You don't require to wait for more than a minute at any given point. An open car, called the dummy, with seats on each side, and four seats at the ends, carries the driver in the centre, and contains levers for the gripping apparatus and the brakes, and there is a close car in the rear for inside passengers. You can go three miles for 3d. I travelled twelve miles over the city in different directions. The drivers and guards are fine-looking men—not like the poor, shabby, over-wrought, under-paid, and badly-used men in Glasgow. I asked one of the drivers how long he worked per day.

"Well," he said, "a little over ten hours—*i.e.*, sixty-three hours per week, and we think it too much. Our pay is £2 14s. 7½d. per week."

If our poor fellows at home had six months of that they would be fatter and fairer than they are. The line, I am told, cost £12,000 a mile to make.

I was looking all day for a drunk man or a beggar, and was just thinking it would be a failure, when I came across a regular old soaker. I saw him twenty yards in advance, standing at a public-house door. I at once reduced my pace that I might have a good look at him. He was a perfect specimen—hands in pockets, blotched face, but cheerful withal. A decent-looking old nigger came past, and Mr. Soaker said laughingly, "Go to ——, you black beggar." The darkie turned a pirouette, and with his open hand gave him one on the cheek. The sound of it made people turn round, and there was my poor countryman falling inwards towards his friend, the publican, while his bonnet rushed over the pavement as if it wanted to catch the car. And my verdict was—served him right.

I went in the evening to St. Kilda station to get a train to the house of my friend, Mr. Aitken, at Albert Park. I was on the platform seven or eight minutes before the time. A young man came up to me and said, " You are Mr. Taylor."

I pled guilty.

He said, " Do you mind of me ? "

It was a puzzler. Taking a careful look at him, I said, " No."

" Well," he replied, " I am an old Kibble boy, and I knew you well when you used to come to the school five or six years ago. My name is Alexander M'Lean. The superintendent of the Kibble will remember me ; I belonged to Greenock, and used to lead the singing for him."

I said : " Come away to a seat till I make some notes, or I will forget your story."

" Oh wait," he said, " till we are in the train."

" No, no, minutes are precious ; and besides, I expect a friend to meet me at the station, and that will interfere with our crack."

He told me he came here six months ago, having learned the trade of compositor in Greenock after leaving the Kibble. He landed in Melbourne with about four shillings, got lodgings in a coffee-shop, and was not successful in getting work till the four shillings were gone. He had to leave his watch with his "uncle" for ten shillings. He met a Scotchman, who said, "Man, can you not take a job at anything till you get one at your own trade?" He replied that he would only be too glad. This man took him to a mason, who engaged him at once as a labourer at seven shillings and sixpence per day. He got work afterwards with a joiner. Another Scotchman said: "Why don't you call on Mr. So-and-so, foreman with Sands & MacDougall, publishers?"

"That's the very man I want," he replied, "and a Greenock man. I knew he was about here, but did not know his address."

He got work at once at the Directory Department, which will not be constant; but he has £2 12s. 6d. per week, out of which he can, and does, save a good deal; and before the present job fails, there is no fear but he will have something else.

The train was busy all the time our conversation was going on. Mr. Aitken was waiting for me at Albert Park. I had to take good-bye with Sandy, wishing him well, and taking a promise from him to come to the ship and see me on the return journey.

Really, it warms one's heart to see one of these boys fairly launched and doing well. He is a member of the Volunteers; and his monthly railway ticket fastened, as is the custom here, to his watch guard. My short interview with this lad has given me more joy than anything else since I left home.

I spent the evening at Mr. Aitken's house, and was introduced to his son and three daughters; also to a Mr. Millar, an old colonial, from the north of Scotland, and a teetotaler. He and I indulged in the dissipation of a smoke. My host told me he had some lady friends coming from the country, adding, " Strange to say, one of them is a Mrs. John Taylor. Won't I have a lark with her when she comes in ? " True enough, the ladies arrived, and I heard him say in the lobby, " What do you think ? We have Peter Taylor here to-night." She came in at once, and was surprised to see a stranger. We had a pleasant conversation, nevertheless, and I found her husband belonged to Perthshire, and, indeed, to my village of Blackford. We had some points in common. She greatly regretted that I would not take time to go inland with her, and see her husband, who lives twenty-five miles away. She said I had the real Taylor complexion.

Tuesday, December 13th.—I went to Melbourne again, and visited the Exhibition buildings and grounds. It is going to be a splendid affair, and Victoria may well be proud of it.

There is one section which shows the pioneer gold-finder. On the left hand is his log shanty, about six feet square; the height of the door is about five feet, and it is hung on leather hinges. Outside is a rude cage made of branches. The fastening of the door is a wooden button about seven inches long, with a nail driven through the centre. There is the figure of a man kneeling, washing earth in a tin basin, to extract the gold-dust. Unknown to him, some aboriginals are watching his doings with no good intent. The whole scene is perfect. You have difficulty in believing the man is not alive. His dress consists of soiled white trowsers, red shirt, and slouched wide-awake; his bare arms and hands are perfect to the life.

Over one circle, at the end of the transept, are the words: " Victoria welcomes all nations; " on the other: " Sing, O Heavens, and be joyful, O Earth." Altogether, I say, " Well done, Victoria! "

I returned to the *Britannia*, after having spent six hours in the city. I like Melbourne better the longer I see it. I can hardly be persuaded, when in company with the people, or listening to the conversation in trains or trams, that I am from home. It is just Scotland, a little refined, if I may say so. English, Irish and Scotch are all mixed up, and the accent is a composite, easily understood by all comers from the old country.

The conductor of the tramway car who gave me particulars of hours and pay, said his father belonged to Glasgow. As far as I see, Scotland predominates.

I find that Mr. F. J. Davis, second officer of this ship, won the twenty-guinea prize for sailor story in *Tit-Bits*, August 14th, 1886. There were 740 competitors for this prize. This gentleman is also author of *Sailor Ballads*, and is altogether a very fine fellow. He has the Bronze Medal of the Royal Humane Society, and a certificate, framed, and hung in his cabin; also a very nice letter from the directors of the P. & O., acknowledging his gallantry. The directors gave him a cheque for £50, as he was disabled for three months through saving a lad at the Albert Docks.

December 16th.—We arrived at Sydney, and were amazed at the prospect of its magnificent harbour.

December 23rd.—Having been advised by many colonials to visit the Janolen Caves, we crossed the

Blue Mountains by the zig-zag railway, and arrived at Tarana, driving thence to Oberon. The road between these two places is somewhat like that between Whiting Bay and Lagg. We passed three ox-teams on the way, with six, seven, and eight yoke respectively.

The altitude at two and a half miles from the caves is 4,400 feet above sea level, but in the two last miles of the journey we descended 1,500 feet. The road would frighten nervous people; it reminded me of the descent of Mount Cenis towards Susa.

We spent about three hours in the Lucas Cave. The crystals are of lime formation; those on the floor are called stalagmites, and those depending from the roof stalactites. The cave is very large. We saw water, with the magnesium light, 70 feet down. A great deal of labour has been expended here; steps have been cut in the solid rock, and certain places have been bridged. Wire rope rails are provided at all dangerous places. I would not attempt to describe the place—one would have to use so many adjectives, and that would be sickening. The formations are as grotesque as could be imagined. There is one cave called the Musical Cave. The guide touched the stalactites of various lengths and produced quite a variety of tones.

Janolen Caves.—Page 226.

> "Here Nature plies her steady task,
>   Vain man, come look upon her,
> The crowd's applause she does not ask—
>   Nor cares for empty honour.
>
> "Such is the lot of mortals, who
>   At Duty's call, each task pursue;
> Good honest work, tho' long concealed,
>   Shall surely stand at last revealed."

There is a bird here which makes a peculiar noise. It is called the laughing jack-ass. A fine is inflicted upon any one for killing it. The reason is that the bird kills the snakes by carrying them up in its bill, and letting them fall.

The following lines are written over the door of the Half-way House, between the caves and Oberon:

> "Since man to man has been unjust,
> I really don't know who to trust;
> I've trusted many, to my sorrow,
> So pay to-day and trust to-morrow."

We left the caves after dinner, 26th December. The water in the creek was right up to the middle the horse's body. We had to stand on the seats of the machine to be dry.

A species of bird, called the *soldier bird*, was pointed out to us on the way. The reason for this name is, that when a snake is seen, four or five of them raise such a row you would think some one was being killed, and this draws attention to the enemy.

December 28th.—We arrived back at Tarana at 10.45. I had a chat with the station-master, who comes from Edinburgh, but has been twenty-four years at this place. I asked how he liked it. He said he *had* to like it, but that it was a dull place, with nothing to break the mono-tony. Pointing to a well-wooded hill, he said, " Every morning when I rise oot o' bed there's that hanged thing staunin' ower there." His name is Mr. Muir. I have his compliments to give to Edinburgh the first time I see it. Sydney was reached at six in the evening.

December 29th.—I am now rolling in an old boat in the direction of Rockymouth, to visit a friend there, Dr. Hood. I did not need any breakfast, and am almost sorry I have come. Summer time is their worst weather here, and I hope we shall not be storm-stayed at Rockymouth.

Hanlan, the great rower, is here, but lying below sick. The smell of the berths—ach!

December 30th.—I arrived at Rockymouth at nine A.M., and was met by Dr. Hood and his assistant. His sisters were also at home. He would not allow me to go to a hotel. The doctor's house is too near the river for health, but the situation is beautiful. He tells me a man can send a horse to grass here for sixpence a week. This is the country for room.

"There's that hanged thing staunin' ower there."

January 1st, 1888.—I am now on board the *City of Grafton,* and expect to be in Sydney at noon. The visit to the doctor was most enjoyable. The steward of this boat tells me the people in the colonies are great gormandisers, and hence the reason so many are sick. There is some truth in it. An old fellow made the attempt twice to sit at table, and was twice defeated. Yesterday, he said the soup was fine—he was twice helped, and had to retreat. To-day, he faced as much fish and sauce as would satisfy a number, and in two seconds there was an absence of daylight till he was out of the staircase.

Butcher meat is consumed in great quantities. Children do not care for milk, and children from the breast have meat minced for them. This is a fine country for the doctors.

A gentleman at table, who employs a number of men, said they all got into bad health. If a bit of skin was chipped from their hands, they would not heal; and the cause, he believed, was they had no meat but mutton for fifteen weeks.

I said, " Had you no bread ? "

" Yes, we had bread; but you can't live on bread."

I entered my dissent modestly, not to give offence.

January 2nd.—I attended a Highland gathering, Sydney, and heard a stump speech from an old fellow, whose nickname is " Garden Honey." He said he was going to stand as Member for the World, and concluded by saying the Autocrat of Russia would one day announce that " Garden Honey " was to be his successor.

January 10th.—I visited, to-day, the Victoria Mint, Melbourne, and saw Mr. George Anderson, the master, late member for Glasgow. We talked of home and Europe, and of Irish affairs. He looked very sage as he said that Gladstone had twice split the Liberal party, and thought it was almost a pity for the world that Gladstone did not die five years ago. He would have gone down to posterity with unsullied name; now it was a tarnished reputation. I listened, and thought with Abraham, " Surely the Judge of all the Earth will do right ! " besides knowing, probably, better than even the master of the Victoria Mint, when Gladstone should be removed.

The public library of this city is magnificent, and its size astonished me.

January 19th.—We left King George's Sound yesterday, at three P.M.. A court-martial was held in the fo'castle to-day, on a dishonest baker. The judges and barristers were in wigs. The sentence was twelve lashes on the bare ——, with a red-hot bar of soap; but on account of the defender's youth, it was mitigated to six. The sentence was duly put into execution.

January 23rd.—

>Every throb of the engine,
>Every turn of the screw,
>Sends the *Britannia* onward
>Nearer to Scotland and you.
>
>Tell the Great Bear to get ready,
>Tell him to trot oot his plough,
>Tell him auld Taylor, the sailor,
>Is watching for them at the bow.
>
>Hurrah for the jolly old skipper!
>Hurrah for the swarthy look-out!
>And hurrah for the Nubian nigger!
>Down in the grime and the soot.
>
>Stuffing the ravenous furnace,
>Smacking its lips at the coal;
>Down goes the Southern Cross,
>And up comes the Northern Pole.
>
>Scotland, auld Scotland, I like ye!
>Wi' a' your sleet and your snaw;
>For hame's hame to the Scottie,
>And dearer the farer awa'!

February 11th.—To-day we drove to the Pyramids. We went through the large one, and entered the sarcophagus in which old Cheops lay. It fits me nicely. In the Khedive's Gardens we heard the Egyptians play—" Ye Banks and Braes," " A Man's a Man for a' That," " Scots Wha Hae," " My Love is like a red red, Rose," " In the Garb of Old Gaul," " Auld Lang Syne," " My Heart is Sair for Somebody," and " Green Grow the Rashes, O."

February 12th.—To-day I went to the museum at Boulac, which is the best of all the Egyptian museums.

How strange to look on the face of old Pharaoh! Poor old chap! he is quiet enough now. One is overpowered by the evidences of Egyptian civilization. Their works of art will compare with any the world has seen. The sarcophagi are wonderful, the workmanship simply perfect, and the hieroglyphics so multifarious that one wonders at the patience they had.

February 13th.—Quite a cavalcade of us went to Memphis to-day. We took train part of the way, and rode afterwards to the statue of Rameses II. Another statue of the same size has also been discovered. The sculpturing of these figures is perfect, and when whole they measured forty-five feet high. As to the mouth, which looked like an ordinary mouth on the figure, I find by a nick I have cut in my stick, that it is over a foot in size across. We went next and saw the tombs of the Sacred Bulls, of which about twenty-five sarcophagi remain. What a work and expense about a bull! I do not wonder after this at the worship of the Golden Calf. I fancy this bullology would then be in universal vogue.

Next we saw the tomb of Tih. The carving on the walls is most elaborate. The oldest pyramid in Egypt or the world is here at Sakarah. It is called the Stepped Pyramid, is built of smaller stones than the others, and looks the worse of the wear. We had lunch in the house of Marriotte of Egyptian fame.

We rode back to the railway, and crossed the Nile in ferry-boat.

February 14th.—We drove to Matareah, and saw the Ostrich Farm. We also saw the fountain Mary is said to have bathed the infant Jesus in, also the sycamore tree under which they rested; next, the Monolith at the Temple of the Sun. Joseph's guidfather was a priest here.

February 15th.—I was first on the top of the pyramid to-day. I had four guides and a doctor to rub my legs. I only wanted three, but all we could say would not keep them back.

One is very much deceived with the size of the pyramids on first seeing them, nor can a proper estimate be formed without going up. The stones which form the outer casing are from two to four feet high. The granite stones in the centre are enormous. One can see the outline of the graveyard from the top of the pyramid, though it cannot be seen when on the ground; a bird's-eye view of the outline of the walls can, however, be traced all round. The guide, as usual, tried to sell me a lot of things on top. I did not buy, but said: "Come down to my dragoman." They did not like that, but I said "I will satisfy you," which pleased them. The Sheik has great power, and seemed a decent fellow. When the men were pressing me to purchase figures, pretending they came out of the tombs, the Sheik warned me they were not genuine.

Great care is taken of people going up. Coming down I gave a hand to each of the two guides, and a turban unwound and tied round my waist was held by a third behind.

The road to the pyramids is most interesting.

We started to-day at half-past seven. The people were coming to town in thousands, and at the Custom-house the crush was frightful. In a few minutes I counted a hundred camels carrying clover of sugar-cane; it would not be an exaggeration to say I met a thousand this morning, and the donkeys would be about three times as numerous. These little creatures amused me. They look so grave, and mean business. They carry nearly as much as the camel. The donkey, meant for riding, is a superior-looking animal. Some good designs can be made in his coat according to how he is cropped.

Gentlemen's carriages have a smart native in uniform running before the carriage to clear the way, which is the Eastern idea of the forerunner. The runner has short trousers coming below the knee, an embroidered jacket and vest, his lower limbs are bare. He is bareheaded, and carries a stick. Some carriages have even two runners.

February 16th.—To-day we went to a Moslem University where they say there are 7,000 scholars.

In the afternoon we drove to two Palaces of the Khedive. We went through the harem of one, but the ladies were absent. If Solomon had more wives than the Khedive, I pity him.

February 17th.—In the afternoon I went to see the dancing and howling dervishes. The former went spinning round at a great speed, and how they can continue so long without getting giddy is a puzzle. The howlers made me think of Elijah and the prophets of Baal; they worked themselves up to such a pitch of excitement that they nearly fainted. It is a queer religious service. The Salvation Army is not in it.

February 18th.—We are now on the road to Suez. We have seen the entrenchments of Tel-el-Kebir, the desert over which our men walked in absolute silence, and the earthworks and fosse over which they leaped, with instructions to cheer and charge.

February 25th.—A Mr. Yorke and his wife, with man-servant and lady's maid, joined the ship at Brindisi, and are going to see their son—a lad at Malta. He is a nice gentleman. He and Richardson, the reader, had a long religious discussion in the smoking-room, Richardson confessing that when amongst Unitarians he was happy, and when amongst Christians he was miserable. Mr. Yorke fenced the Bible difficulties, and latterly I took part, and astonished Mr. Richardson by boldly stating I believed in the passage of the Red Sea by the Israelites. It seems to be a common point with a great many intelligent travellers to deny the divinity of Christ. I have made a stand for it. A Mr. Jennings, whose company I have enjoyed, said to me to-day, "You never find Christ claiming it."

I answered very politely: "Well, Mr. Jennings, I have not read to the same conclusion as you. In the intercessory prayer of our Lord, He says—'And now, O Father, glorify Thou Me with the glory which I had with Thee before the world was.' That surely goes far back into a past eternity," I said.

It made a slight impression; he said he would not for the world be the means of unsettling by a hair's-breadth the faith of any man.

February 27th.—We left Malta Monday 11.30, with Prince George of Wales on board, going home to his father's silver wedding.

I sit at table opposite an old gentleman called Mr. Grant, an Indian indigo planter. He tells me he brought up his son to be an indigo broker, but, as the latter has a conscience, he would not be a broker, and said to his father he would grow the indigo and let others sell it. The old man has travelled between India and home forty-seven times.

The chief engineer is a Mr. Philips, and used to be in Thomson's of Clydebank, where I also was.

As already mentioned, the Prince of Wales' second son is a passenger. I was amused at the preparations to receive him. All the officers got on their surtouts and buttons—the first officer at the ladder, with the best pair of sea legs in the ship, though they could not stop a pig in an entry. The Prince, dressed in a brown felt and an ulster, came round to the other side in a boat and up the ladder, and was walking up and down amongst those waiting for him before they knew. He is a nice-looking young man, and sits at our table, a little on the left and at the opposite side, so that I can see him well.

February 28th.—I went down to tea at four P.M. One of the tables was full, not a seat to be had at it. Prince George was at another, with about half-a-dozen cups spread about him. I sat down opposite and boldly laid hold of the common tea-pot, from which he was drinking, and helped myself. He did not speak—neither did I. But had he known that twenty-five years before I sat up most of the night, when I should have been sleeping, making two royal crowns in honour of his father and mother out of *twa auld barrel-hoops*—the which, when dressed with green leaves and flowers by my wife's hands, were fit for the blood royal, and looked well among other floral decorations at Kadikoi Place, Kilmarnock, on March 10th, 1863—had he known that, I say, he might have vouchsafed me a word.

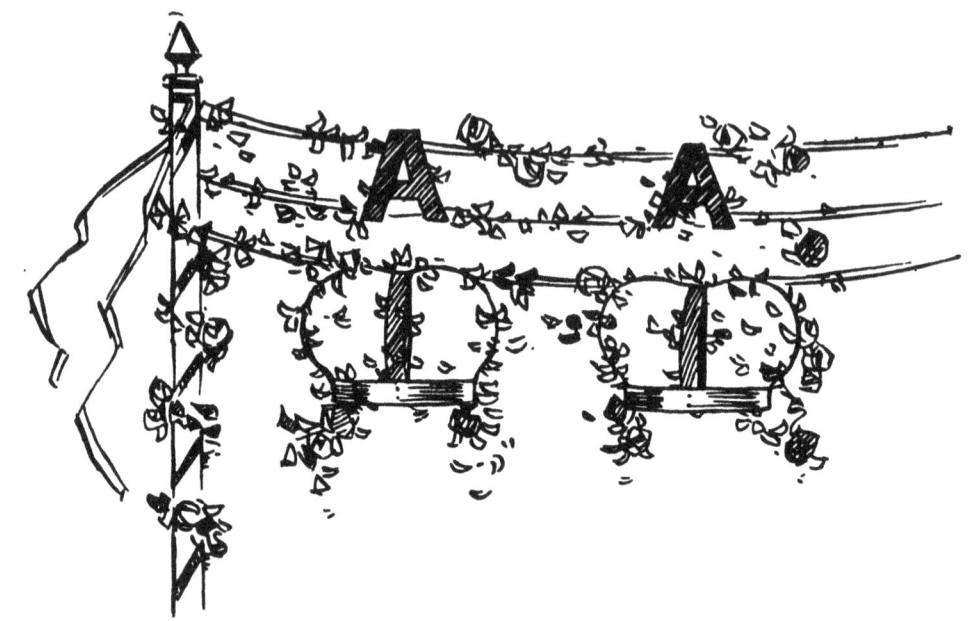

March 10th, 1863.

March 1st.—Last night we had two songs and a recitation. The captain gave "The Crew of the Captain's Gig." Mr. Locke Richardson recited us "Enoch Arden." This gentleman is an American from Canada, I think. He is an accomplished reader—tender and quiet, with no stage thunder. He was particularly touching when delineating the three children, Enoch, Philip, and Annie. I was very much pleased with him and Tennyson.

We have an Irishman here—a Mr. Allen—who gave us an Irish piece the other night, on money, harmony, and matrimony, full of Irish bulls. He brought in a story about Ould Lantie, who had a wooden leg, and who, when going home one dark night in Dublin, put his pin in a fire plug and walked in a circle till daylight, flourishing his latch-key and asking who stole " My hall-door."

March 3rd.—We are now in the Bay of Biscay, and last night was ugly in the extreme. Seven hundred and eighty miles are between us and Plymouth. The person next me at table is down on our education in England, which he says is spoiling even the domestic servants. "The first question a domestic puts is : ' How often will I have my night out ?' If she is told, ' Once a month,' she will reply, 'No, I must have it once a fortnight.' And some have the impertinence to say once a week." I turned on him like a Bashi-Bazouk, and said, " Why not ? People who would only grant a few hours to a servant once a month don't deserve one." He changed the subject.

March 5th.—We are still in the Bay of Biscay, but the water now is as smooth as the Indian Ocean.

The day is warm and pleasant. We hope to be in Plymouth to-morrow early, and I hope to proceed to London by first train, and leave at night for home. *The P. & O. owe me nothing. I consider I have got good value for my £105. Their servants have used me well, and I respect them all.*

March 6th.—We passed the Eddystone Lighthouse this morning at 4 A.M.

I had breakfast with Prince George of Wales this morning. I sat next him, and ventured to say, " This is an early start, sir."

" By, I should rather think so," he replied.

CONCLUSION

Much has happened since the morning I parted from Royalty at Plymouth, of which as yet it is not meet to write. Advancing years bring us no nearer the solution of the great problem of life. Still, I think it well worth living, even in the humblest sphere, if we try to live it worthily. The importance of humanity may be assumed from the fact that in every soul there is a variety of voices continually wooing us in diverse directions; and the great decision, though come to in some crisis of the soul, has to be renewed and re-affirmed day after day so long as we are here.

The claims of religion are not more exacting than those of merely mundane things, while the rewards of the latter are less. The Christian is called upon to forsake all and follow his Master. The aspirant to earthly distinction gets off no easier if he would succeed. To both it is equally true: "Strait is the gate and narrow is the way that leadeth unto life and few there be that find it." How many have we all seen striving, even agonising, to enter the earthly portal, and have not been able; and one pitiful aspect of life is, that no matter what the bent of the mind may be, one half of existence and often the whole, must be devoted to a life-and-death struggle with hunger. The wolf, though beaten from the door time and again, bears a charmed life and always returns. And while some have so entrenched themselves as to feel safe, nevertheless when they begin to take stock it is with shame they discover that they have little else *but the struggle* to show for a life of three score years and ten.

www.ingramcontent.com/pod-product-compliance
Lightning Source LLC
Chambersburg PA
CBHW081324090426
42737CB00017B/3023